ACKNOWLEDGEMENTS

In compiling this book I have been greatly helped by many organisations, fellow enthusiasts and friends. The official British Rail photographs have been reproduced by courtesy of the BR/OPC Joint Venture. John Edgington, Technical Information Officer, and C. P. Atkins, Librarian, at the National Railway Museum, York, have been most helpful in providing information from Museum sources. Alan Gettings, whose etched nameplates for modellers are works of art in miniature, kindly provided the drawings and information on the numbers and various plates carried by the Standard engines, in addition to answering numerous questions. Last but by no means least, many photographers, whose work is separately credited, kindly made their work available and often went to great trouble to provide pictures of particular subjects. To all these gentlemen I extend my sincere thanks.

Printed in the City of Oxford

Typeset by Aquarius Typsetting Services

Published by:
Oxford Publishing Co.
Link House,
West Street,
Poole,
Dorset.

Contents

Introduction

The range of Standard steam engines introduced by British Railways in 1951 represented the ultimate development of the steam locomotive in Great Britain. While on the whole they showed no advance in power over the designs of the four companies which preceded the nationalised British Railways, they were far better suited to the economic and social conditions of the immediate post-war years. In that period of austerity, neither the finance nor the materials were available for a massive re-equipment programme or for the large-scale electrification. The diesel locomotive was still in its infancy, though its suitability for shunting was clearly recognised and the decision to produce standard steam engines was wholly wise in the prevailing circumstances. But the golden years of the 1930s when complicated locomotives were produced in the confidence that they would be properly driven and maintained by a competent work-force, and supplied with good coal, were gone. Now there was a need for locomotives which required the minimum of attention and were economical irrespective of the quality of fuel. At the same time there was an awareness of the arduous conditions of work associated with steam, not only in driving and firing engines in all weathers on the road but in servicing and repairing them at sheds, often in primitive surroundings. These conditions had to be improved if men were to be attracted to work on the railways in competition with more congenial and perhaps more lucrative jobs elsewhere.

Therefore the new Standard engines were designed to meet the requirements of the times – to be cheap to build, to work economically at their intended power outputs, to be convenient to drive and fire, to cover greater mileages between major overhauls and to be easy to service and repair. The 'Britannia', for example, though no more powerful than the various multi-cylinder engines of the four companies, was a far more practical machine, with its two cylinders, sturdy frame, large boiler and wide firebox, than the three-cylinder 'Royal Scot', the various Gresley designs, the four-cylinder 'Castle' of 1923 vintage and the expensively erratic Bulleid Pacifics, and the same sort of superiority was achieved throughout the range. The LMS had had the same aims in the development of its modern classes but this was the first time that engines to suit every duty had been designed on these lines. Indeed, it was the first time in Great Britain that engineers had had the opportunity to start afresh and design a complete range of engines.

The BR Standard engines were designed under the overall supervision of R. A. Riddles, member of the Railway Executive for mechanical and electrical engineering. Responsible to him were the Chief Officer (Locomotive Construction and Maintenance), R. C. Bond, and the Executive Officer (Design), E. S. Cox, who thus was largely responsible for actually designing the new locomotives. This team of three men all came from the LMS and it was to be expected that LMS influences should be seen in the Standard engines. It was, moreover, right that this was so. The LMS had produced standard engines which were equally at home as far afield as Bournemouth and Wick and under its last Chief Mechanical Engineer, H. G. Ivatt, it had done more than any other company to adapt the steam locomotive to the changed conditions of the post-war world. Ivatt had built on the foundations laid by Stanier, who had imported the excellent practices of the GWR to the LMS in the 1930s. So the BR Standard engines were the ultimate development of the tradition which had its origins in the classic work of Churchward at the turn of the century.

The range of twelve Standard classes was planned to meet the whole of the traffic requirements of British Railways. It comprised nine tender and three tank engine classes. No provision was made for a standard shunting engine, that duty having already been assigned to the diesel. Work began on producing ten of the twelve classes straightaway but two were delayed as there was no immediate need for them. The four companies had an adequate stock of Class 8 express engines for the needs of the 1950s and in the event the prototype Class 8, No. 71000 was the only engine ever produced by BR in that category. Similarly, there were ample Class 8 heavy freight engines available, thanks to the large numbers of Stanier Class 8F 2-8-0s, WD 2-8-0s and WD 2-10-0s built for war needs. So no BR Standard 8F 2-8-0 was ever planned or contemplated and the designers opted for the increased performance of a 9F from the outset. Of the twelve classes five were based very closely on LMS designs, the Class 5 4-6-0, the Class 4 2-6-0 and 2-6-4T, and the Class 2 2-6-0 and 2-6-2T. The three Pacific classes, the Class 9F 2-10-0, the Class 4 4-6-0 and the Class 3 2-6-0 and 2-6-2T were all new designs. All classes had the same range of standard parts and detail fittings, and great care was taken to choose the best from what was available both from the old companies' designs and from private industry.

The BR range of twelve Standard classes makes an interesting comparison with the LMS Standard range, announced in 1947, of eight classes (not including three classes of shunters, one of them diesel). By comparison with the LMS, BR had too small a difference between its classes and so had four more than necessary, the Class 6 4-6-2, Class 4 4-6-0, Class 3 2-6-0 and Class 3 2-6-2T. The BR system was, of course, considerably bigger than the LMS and a greater number of classes could perhaps be justified on those grounds alone. Two of the extra four classes were originally built for the Western Region, the Class 4 4-6-0, which was intended for the same jobs as the GWR 'Manor', on lines where a Class 5 was prohibited for reasons of weight, and the Class 3 2-6-2T. On the LMS the duties of the former would have been performed by the Class 4 2-6-0 and of the latter by the Class 4 2-6-4T or, if a lighter locomotive was needed, by the Class 2 2-6-2T. Whether the additional classes were really required, however, is now a matter for idle speculation and hindsight, but certainly two of them were the smallest of all the BR classes proper, the Class 6 4-6-2 and the Class 3 2-6-0.

There is little doubt, however, about the most successful of the Standard classes. The 9F 2-10-0 was the one class which represented an advance in power over the engines it displaced, being considerably superior in freight haulage to the various 8F 2-8-0s. Moreover, these remarkable engines were found to be equally at home on express passenger trains, on such different routes as the Somerset & Dorset and the Great Northern main line, where one was timed at 90 mph. The BR management was as surprised by this as anyone and eventually prohibited them from exceeding 60 mph.

One of the principles on which the BR Standards were designed was that every part which might need attention should be readily accessible and so fittings which engineers in the past had discreetly hidden away, irrespective of any problems so caused for the men who worked on their engines, were now plainly visible. Another factor which had a considerable effect on their appearance was the high position of the running plate. E. S. Cox took the view that as an engine's boiler was immensely strong and rigid, many components such as the cab, running plate and injectors were best secured directly to it.

This would avoid problems caused by differential movement, vibration and expansion, when these parts were attached partly to the frames and partly to the boiler. The running plate was therefore much higher than on a conventional British engine in which it was attached to the frames, but nevertheless a conscious effort was made to present a tidy appearance. No unsightly gap was left in front of the cylinders, as had occurred on Riddles' WD locomotives and on Ivatt's last designs for the LMS. Instead, the gap was closed by sweeping the running plate straight down at a steep angle to join that behind the buffer beam and the same lines were complemented at the other end of the engine, except on the Pacifics, by 'cutting away' the lower front corner of the cab. In this way the Standard engines were given an appearance which made them seem different from everything that had gone before, which stamped them all with a family likeness, and which disguised their LMS ancestry.

Although the configuration of the running plate was quite new on a British engine, it had long been seen abroad, in such countries as the United States, Germany, South Africa and Japan. What was different about the BR arrangement was that when seen from the side it was much deeper than elsewhere. This was done deliberately, as, unlike the over-seas engines which had sundry pipework running along their boilers, the BR Standards had such pipework fastened beneath the running plate. There, thanks to the deep sides, it was hidden from the public gaze but still remained accessible for maintenance. This largely accounts for the clean lines of the boilers of all the Standard engines. So, despite their basically functional approach, the designers of the last British steam engines were still concerned to give thought to appearance. The same sort of attention was paid to chimneys. After Riddles' WD engines, stovepipes might have been expected but in fact an

attractive range was produced for the various classes which was wholly in keeping with British traditions.

With their generally clean lines, the **BR Standards** had a tidy workmanlike air. They were not beautiful by the criteria of the Victorian designers or even by those of the 1920s or 1930s (though the old saying that beauty is in the eye of the beholder is as true of locomotives as of anything) but they had an appeal and attractiveness of their own. Certainly, the Pacifics and 2-10-0s were imposing machines, the strong lines of the running plate being matched by the large high-pitched boilers, and the Class 4 2-6-4 tank engines were attractive too, with their stylishly curved side-tanks. On some of the smaller engines, however, the running plate was an over-dominant feature, especially where it was steeply inclined at the smokebox. It emphasised the long and spindly look of the Class 4 4-6-0 and upset the balance of the Class 4 and 3 2-6-0s, which were otherwise neat modern designs. The two Class 2 designs did not suffer in this respect. They had the lower and thinner running plate of their LMS predecessors but improved upon them by having the gap in front of the cylinders closed with plating at the same angle as the other **BR** classes.

The purpose of this book is to present a record of these engines in photographs and drawings, both when they were new and in service. All the main variations in external appearance are described, along with the majority of the minor ones.

E. Talbot
Stafford
August 1982

BRITISH RAILWAYS

TYPES OF LOCOMOTIVES REPRODUCED TO THE SAME SCALE

CLASS 7 – SERIES 70000
Type 4-6-2   6ft. 2in. Wheels
Total Weight 143 tons 3 cwt. – T.E. 32150 (lb)

CLASS 4 – SERIES 75000
Type 4-6-0   5ft. 8in. Wheels
Total Weight 119 tons 3 cwt. – T.E. 25515 (lb)

CLASS 3 – SERIES 77000
Type 2-6-0   5ft. 3in. Wheels
Total Weight 99 tons 13 cwt. – T.E. 21490 (lb)

CLASS 2 – SERIES 84000
Type 2-6-2T   5ft. 0in. Wheels
Total Weight 66 tons 5 cwt. – T.E. 18513 (lb)

CLASS 8 – SERIES 71000
Type 4-6-2   6ft. 2in. Wheels
Total Weight 156 tons 16 cwt. – T.E. 39080 (lb)

CLASS 5 – SERIES 73000
Type 4-6-0   6ft. 2in. Wheels
Total Weight 125 tons 3 cwt. – T.E. 26120 (lb)

CLASS 4 – SERIES 80000
Type 2-6-4T   5ft. 8in. Wheels
Total Weight 86 tons 13 cwt. – T.E. 25515 (lb)

CLASS 3 – SERIES 82000
Type 2-6-2T   5ft. 3in. Wheels
Total Weight 74 tons 1 cwt. – T.E. 21490 (lb)

CLASS 9 – SERIES 92000
Type 2-10-0   5ft. 0in. Wheels
Total Weight 139 tons 4 cwt. – T.E. 39667 (lb)

CLASS 6 – SERIES 72000
Type 4-6-2   6ft. 2in. Wheels
Total Weight 137 tons 13 cwt. – T.E. 27520 (lb)

CLASS 4 – SERIES 76000
Type 2-6-0   5ft. 3in. Wheels
Total Weight 101 tons 18 cwt. – T.E. 24170 (lb)

CLASS 2 – SERIES 78000
Type 2-6-0   5ft. 0in. Wheels
Total Weight 86 tons 2 cwt. – T.E. 18513 (lb)

Part One

BRITISH RAILWAYS STANDARD LOCOMOTIVE SURVEY

'BRITANNIA'
CLASS 7, 4-6-2,
Tender Engines
Nos. 70000 ~ 70054

Plate 1 The first BR Standard engine to be completed was No. 70000 *Britannia* in January 1951. After working trials between Crewe and Carlisle in plain black livery and without nameplates, No. 70000 re-entered Crewe Works to be painted in the standard livery of Brunswick green with orange and black lining and to have nameplates fitted. It is seen here at Crewe before dispatch to Marylebone for the naming ceremony, performed by the Minister of Transport, Alfred Barnes, on 31st January, 1951.   *British Rail*

Plate 2 Drawing for 'Britannias' Nos. 70000-44, except that Nos. 70025-9 had BR 1A tenders holding 5,000 gallons of water.

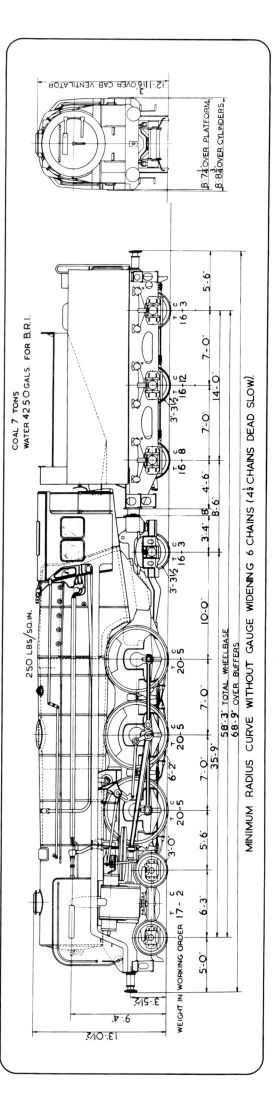

COAL 7 TONS
WATER 4250 GALS. FOR B.R.I.

250 LBS/SQ.IN.

WEIGHT IN WORKING ORDER

MINIMUM RADIUS CURVE WITHOUT GAUGE WIDENING 6 CHAINS (4½ CHAINS DEAD SLOW)

Plate 3 No. 70004 *William Shakespeare* was given a special 'exhibition finish' for display at the 1951 Festival of Britain exhibition. Many parts were chromium-plated, copper pipes were polished and brass fittings burnished. The special finish clearly shows the hollow axles of the original design. All the first 25 engines were temporarily withdrawn in October 1951 after trouble with driving wheels shifting on axles. Part of the cure was the plugging of the axle ends for the distance of the wheel seats. *British Rail*

Plate 4 Eight of the first batch of 'Britannias' were allocated to the Western Region. Here, No. 70019 *Lightning* is seen in original condition at Swindon soon after delivery from Crewe. It is already fitted with WR lamp irons. *British Rail.*

Plate 5 All the early Standard engines had tenders with the coal space inset in the same fashion as Riddles' War Department 2-8-0s and 2-10-0s and Ivatt's LMS Class 4F and 2F 2-6-0s. The reason was to provide better visibility when running tender first but in practice little use was made of this feature with the 'Britannias', which were predominantly employed on express-passenger work despite their mixed-traffic classification. Flexible screens were fitted between engine and tender as a modification to the original design after complaints from crews about draughty cabs, but these screens were only partly effective. This view was taken to record the second **BR** emblem first applied to No.

70016 and displayed at Marylebone on 21st June, 1956. At first the new emblem was produced in two forms, one with the lion facing to the left and the other with it facing right, so that it would be facing towards the front on both sides of the locomotive. However, since the emblem with the lion facing left was the one approved by the College of Heralds, it was ruled in late 1959 that only that form should be used. So henceforth the lion on the right-hand side of locomotives faced backwards.

British Rail

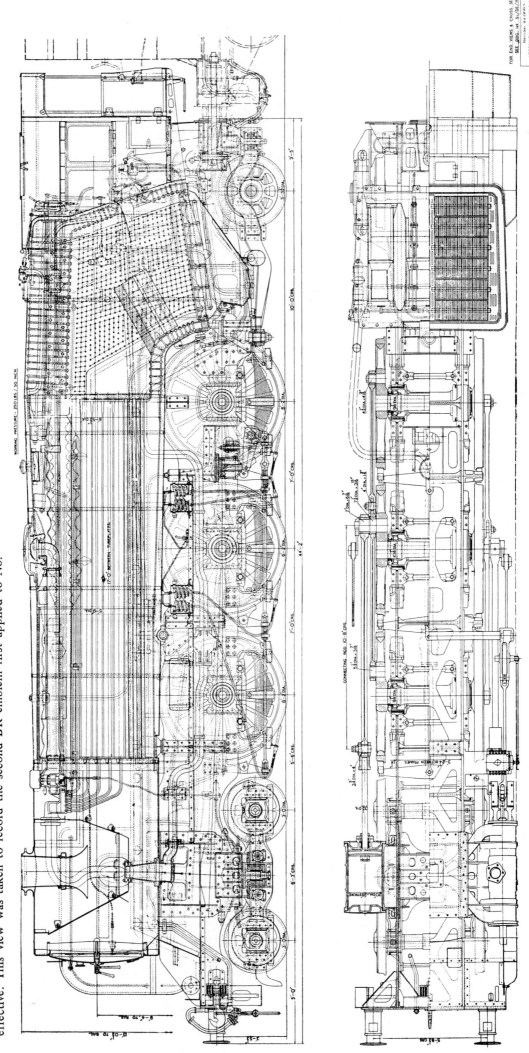

GENERAL ARRANGEMENT - CLASS 7. 4-6-2 TENDER ENGINE.
ELEVATION & PLAN

Plate 6 General arrangement of No. 70000.

Plate 7 After the Didcot accident of 20th November, 1955, when No. 70026 *Polar Star* was derailed, the view ahead from the 'Britannia' cab was improved by removing the hand-rails from the smoke deflectors and, on the Western Region ones only, lowering the ejector exhaust pipe (alongside the smokebox). This view of No. 70023 *Venus* shows the Swindon modification of the smoke deflectors, with six rectangular hand-holds. By comparison with the view of *Lightning (Plate 4)*, a number of other modifications have occurred in the intervening five years: a single wide footstep under the smokebox instead of two small ones, a rectangular-section leading coupling rod instead of fluted, footplating cut away to give access to the lubricator, draught screens between engine and tender, a footstep on the rear of the tender, to facilitate filling the tank, and the second type of BR emblem.

British Rail

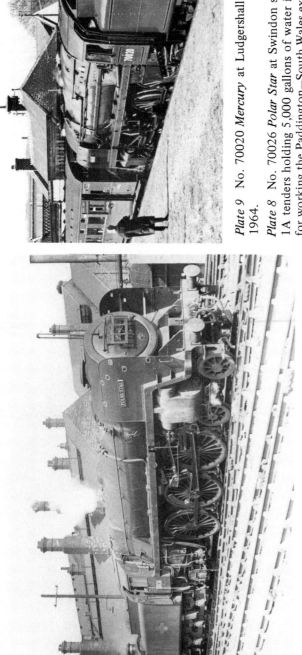

Plate 9 No. 70020 *Mercury* at Ludgershall with an enthusiasts' special on 8th February, 1964.

Hugh Ballantyne

Plate 8 No. 70026 *Polar Star* at Swindon shed about 1960. The 70025-9 batch had BR 1A tenders holding 5,000 gallons of water instead of the 4,250 gallons of the BR 1 type, for working the Paddington—South Wales expresses.

J.H. Russell

Plate 10 A later view of No. 70026 *Polar Star*, in Crewe Works after overhaul. After being displaced by diesels, the Western Region's 'Britannias' were transferred to the London Midland Region, hence the 6J shedplate (Holyhead) on No. 70026. *J.B. Bucknall*

Plate 11 No. 70037 *Hereward the Wake* at March shed in March 1961. The 'Britannias' brought new standards of performance to the main-line services out of Liverpool Street.

J.H. Russell

Plate 12 No. 70025 *Western Star* at Crewe North on 21st March, 1964, after transfer from the Western Region to the London Midland. It has LMR lamp irons, the top one being lowered for safety reasons because of electrification. The AWS apparatus beneath the buffer beam is protected by a steel plate from damage by the coupling and the associated equipment is housed in the battery box and cylinder on the right-hand running plate.

Author

Plate 13 One of the second batch of 'Britannias', No. 70030 *William Wordsworth*, as built in November 1952. It has rectangular-section coupling rods, smaller driving-wheel balance weights and a larger dome than the original version. The small boxes on the running plate are the modified covers of the sandboxes.

British Rail

Plate 14 No. 70032 *Tennyson* at Stafford with an up parcels train about 1963. Above the figure '2' of the engine number on the cab-side is the slot for the driver's name, a feature introduced in mid-1956 for engines on the main expresses but never widely or regularly used. The smoke deflectors have still not been modified with hand-holds instead of rails, this alteration being applied very slowly except on the Western Region.

J.B. Bucknall

Plate 15 The last two of the second batch, Nos. 70043-4, were built new with air brakes for comparative trials between vacuum- and air-braked freight trains. Apart from alterations necessitated by the fitting of air compressors, such as the absence of smoke deflectors, these two engines were standard with the rest of the second batch. No. 70044 is seen here as built. *British Rail*

Plate 16 On completion of the trials, the air-brake equipment was removed from Nos. 70043-4 and smoke deflectors and nameplates were fitted as usual for the class. No. 70044 *Earl Haig* is seen here at Crewe North shed on 7th June, 1963. As well as the usual detail alterations, it has the Crewe version of the smoke-deflector modification and a speedometer driven off the rear driving wheel. The mounting of the return crank' has also been modified. It is now secured by four studs, as in standard LMS practice, instead of being mounted on a square pin (LNER-style). This modification first appeared on Pacifics in August 1956, when Nos. 70052/54 and 72000 were so fitted. *Author*

BRITISH RAILWAYS STANDARD, CLASS 7, 4-6-2 *Tender Engine*

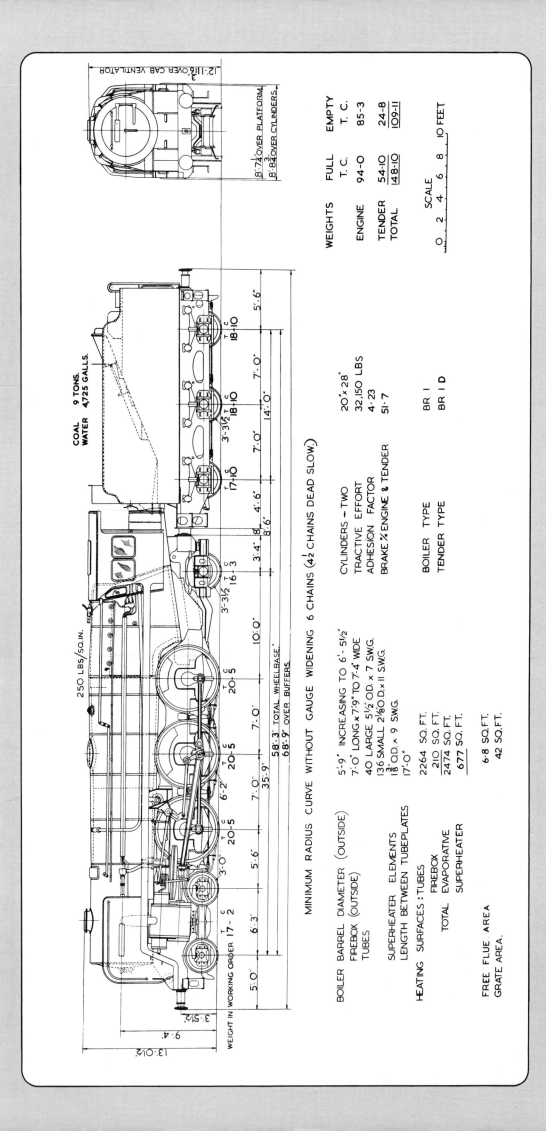

WEIGHTS

	FULL T.C.	EMPTY T.C.
ENGINE	94·0	85·3
TENDER	54·10	24·8
TOTAL	148·10	109·11

SCALE

0 2 4 6 8 10 FEET

12'·11⅝ OVER CAB VENTILATOR

8'·7¼ OVER PLATFORM
8'·8¼ OVER CYLINDERS

COAL 9 TONS.
WATER 4,725 GALLS.

250 LBS/SQ.IN.

MINIMUM RADIUS CURVE WITHOUT GAUGE WIDENING 6 CHAINS (4½ CHAINS DEAD SLOW.)

WEIGHT IN WORKING ORDER

CYLINDERS – TWO	20 × 28"
TRACTIVE EFFORT	32,150 LBS
ADHESION FACTOR	4·23
BRAKE % ENGINE & TENDER	51·7
BOILER TYPE	BR 1
TENDER TYPE	BR 1 D

BOILER BARREL DIAMETER (OUTSIDE)	5'-9" INCREASING TO 6'- 5½"
FIREBOX (OUTSIDE)	7'·0" LONG × 7'·9" TO 7'·4" WIDE
TUBES	40 LARGE 5½" OD × 7 SWG.
	136 SMALL 2⅛" O.D. × 11 SWG.
SUPERHEATER ELEMENTS	1⅜" O.D. × 9 SWG.
LENGTH BETWEEN TUBEPLATES	17'·0"
HEATING SURFACES : TUBES	2264 SQ. FT.
FIREBOX	210 SQ. FT.
TOTAL EVAPORATIVE	2474 SQ. FT.
SUPERHEATER	677 SQ. FT.
FREE FLUE AREA	6·8 SQ.FT.
GRATE AREA.	42 SQ.FT.

Plate 17 Drawing for the last batch of 'Britannias', Nos. 70045-54. These engines had the modified cab layout, with gangway doors attached to the tender and a grab-rail on the tender of roughly the same height as the doors, as on No. 71000.

Plate 20 The only un-named **BR** Standard Pacific (and only the second un-named British Pacific, after **LMS** No. 6202) was No. 70047, seen here standing near Bangor No. 2 signal box in June 1963. Detail of the grab-rail on the front of the tender and of the modified trailing axle-box cover is clearly shown.

E. N. Kneale

Plate 18 A fine view of the first of the last batch of 'Britannias', No. 70045 *Lord Rowallan*, taken after the engine had been prepared for naming, in July 1957, some three years after completion. It has all the modifications usual by that time. The tender is type **BR 1D**, carrying 9 tons of coal and 4,725 gallons of water. In place of the inset coal space of type **BR 1**, it has flush sides with a high curved top, similar to **LMS** practice, and is fitted with a coal pusher. The only other British tenders so equipped were those of the Stanier 'Coronation' Class Pacifics and of the lone BR Class 8P Pacific No. 71000 *Duke of Gloucester*.

British Rail

Plate 19 The nameplate of No. 70045, which was named after the Chief Scout on 16th July, 1957. This locomotive was used on 1st August to haul the train taking the Chief Scout from St. Pancras to Sutton Park for the opening of the World Scout Jamboree. For some reason, the LMR was very slow to name its allocation of five of the last batch and No. 70047 was never named. Originally, the background of BR nameplates was painted red but in mid-1952 it was announced that 'as a result of experience, and with the object of greater legibility, black is to be adopted instead'. This seems, however, to have been something in which complete standardisation was never achieved. *British Rail*

LORD ROWALLAN

Plate 21 No. 70048 *The Territorial Army 1908-1958* photographed here in July 1958.
British Rail

Plate 22 The last of the 'Britannias' to be built, No. 70054 *Dornoch Firth*, at Crewe Works after overhaul in the early 1960s. It has acquired a single wide footstep under the smokebox, electrification warning flashes and AWS equipment. The Timken roller-bearing axleboxes of the trailing truck and tender are painted yellow with a horizontal red stripe.

J.B. Bucknall

Plate 23 The front end of No. 70048, photographed in July 1958. This batch was fitted from new with many of the modifications applied to the previous batches after they had been in service for some time. Seen here is the lower position of the vacuum pipe (on the right of the engine) by comparison with the earliest members of the class but the single wide footstep beneath the smokebox is a later modification, even the last batch having two small ones when new. The 'SC' plate on the smokebox door signifies 'self-cleaning' smokebox.

British Rail

ARRANGEMENT OF CAB FITTINGS

FIREMAN'S SIDE.

DRIVER'S SIDE.

STEAM MANIFOLD MAIN SHUT-OFF VALVE.

WATER GAUGES.

CARRIAGE WARMING PRESSURE GAUGE.

CARRIAGE WARMING REDUCING VALVE.

BOILER PRESSURE GAUGE.

FIREHOLE DOORS.

EXHAUST STEAM INJECTOR STEAM VALVE.

LIVE STEAM INJECTOR STEAM VALVE.

EXHAUST STEAM INJECTOR FEED WATER VALVE.

COAL WATERING COCK.

TENDER SPRINKLER VALVE.

DAMPER CONTROL.

LIVE STEAM INJECTOR FEED WATER VALVE.

ROCKING GRATE LEVERS.

CYLINDER OIL INDICATOR.

STEAM CHEST PRESSURE GAUGE.

VACUUM GAUGE.

WHISTLE VALVE HANDLE.

GRADUABLE STEAM BRAKE VALVE.

DRIVER'S BRAKE VALVE, VACUUM RELIEF VALVE, & RELEASE VALVE.

REGULATOR.

SMALL EJECTOR STEAM VALVE.

LARGE EJECTOR STEAM VALVE.

BLOWER VALVE.

REVERSING GEAR.

CYLINDER COCK OPERATING HANDLE.

SANDING VALVE.

STEAM BRAKE LUBRICATOR.

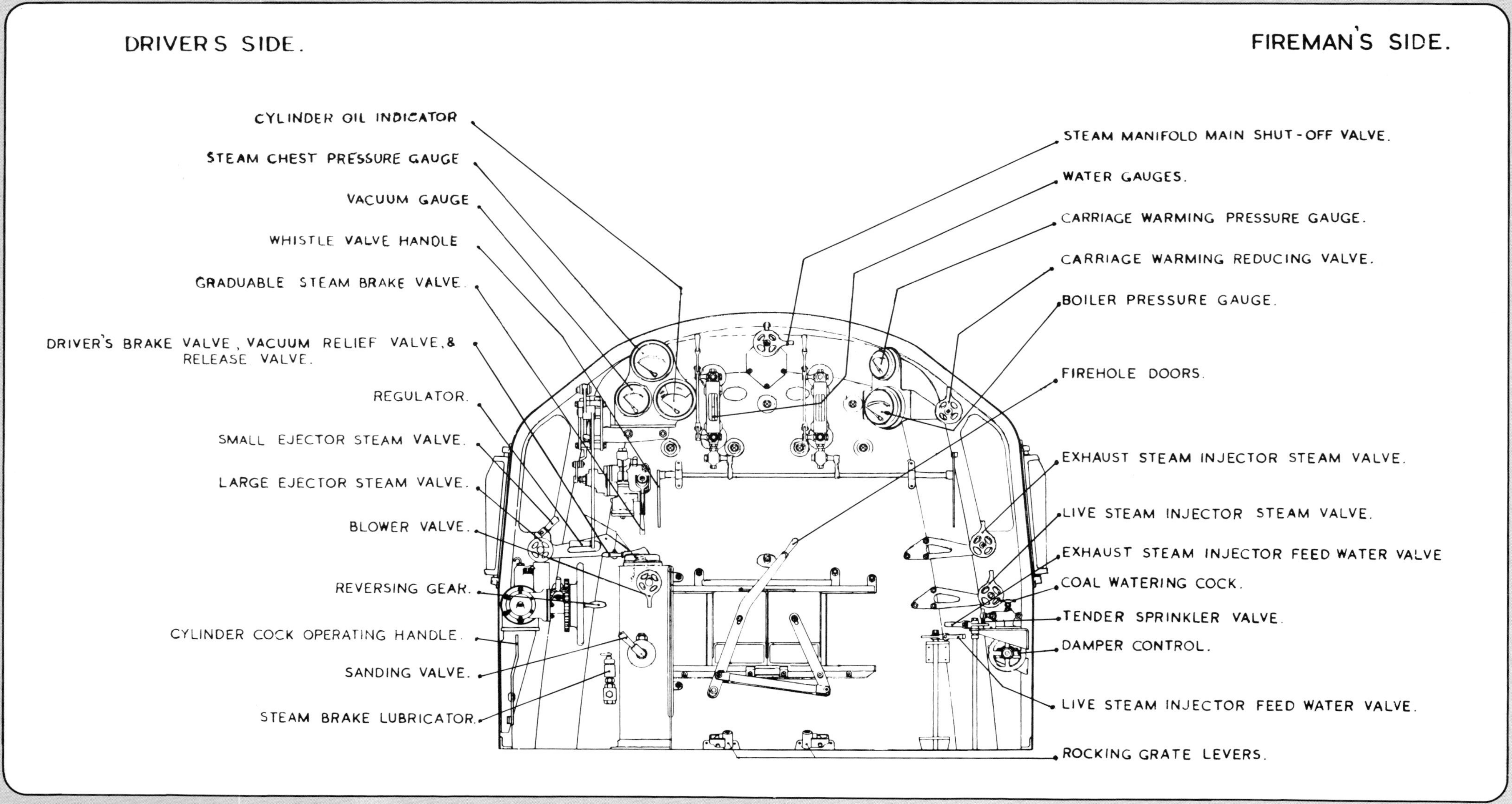

Plate 24 Arrangement of cab fittings.

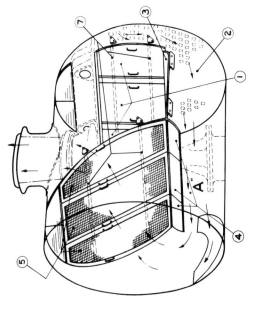

Plate 26

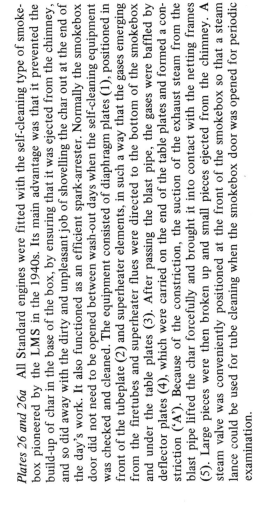

TYPICAL SELF CLEANING SMOKEBOX

Plate 26a

Plate 25 Cab end view of No. 70000 showing the injectors and other fittings attached to the boiler. The locomotive is as first turned out of Crewe Works, in plain black livery, before returning after trials to be repainted in the standard lined green.

Plates 26 and 26a All Standard engines were fitted with the self-cleaning type of smokebox pioneered by the LMS in the 1940s. Its main advantage was that it prevented the build-up of char in the base of the box, by ensuring that it was ejected from the chimney, and so did away with the dirty and unpleasant job of shovelling the char out at the end of the day's work. It also functioned as an efficient spark-arrester. Normally the smokebox door did not need to be opened between wash-out days when the self-cleaning equipment was checked and cleaned. The equipment consisted of diaphragm plates (1), positioned in front of the tubeplate (2) and superheater elements, in such a way that the gases emerging from the firetubes and superheater flues were directed to the bottom of the smokebox and under the table plates (3). After passing the blast pipe, the gases were baffled by deflector plates (4), which were carried on the end of the table plates and formed a constriction ('A'). Because of the constriction, the suction of the exhaust steam from the blast pipe lifted the char forcefully and brought it into contact with the netting frames (5). Large pieces were then broken up and small pieces ejected from the chimney. A steam valve was conveniently positioned at the front of the smokebox so that a steam lance could be used for tube cleaning when the smokebox door was opened for periodic examination.

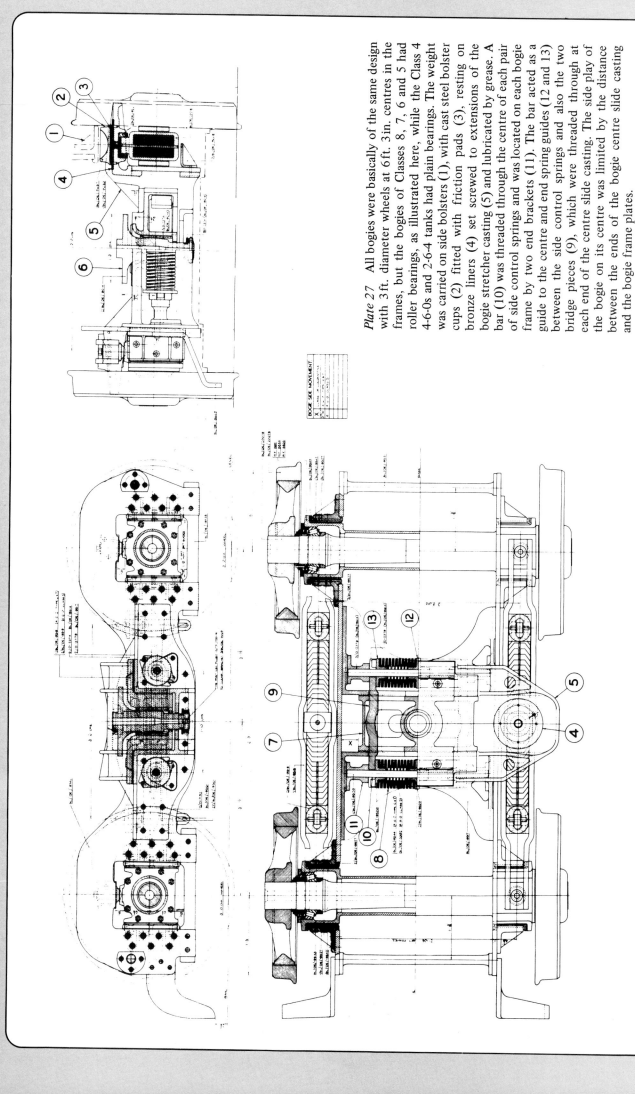

Plate 27 All bogies were basically of the same design with 3ft. diameter wheels at 6ft. 3in. centres in the frames, but the bogies of Classes 8, 7, 6 and 5 had roller bearings, as illustrated here, while the Class 4 4-6-0s and 2-6-4 tanks had plain bearings. The weight was carried on side bolsters (1), with cast steel bolster cups (2) fitted with friction pads (3), resting on bronze liners (4) set screwed to extensions of the bogie stretcher casting (5) and lubricated by grease. A bar (10) was threaded through the centre of each pair of side control springs and was located on each bogie frame by two end brackets (11). The bar acted as a guide to the centre and end spring guides (12 and 13) between the side control springs and also the two bridge pieces (9), which were threaded through at each end of the centre slide casting. The side play of the bogie on its centre was limited by the distance between the ends of the bogie centre slide casting and the bogie frame plates.

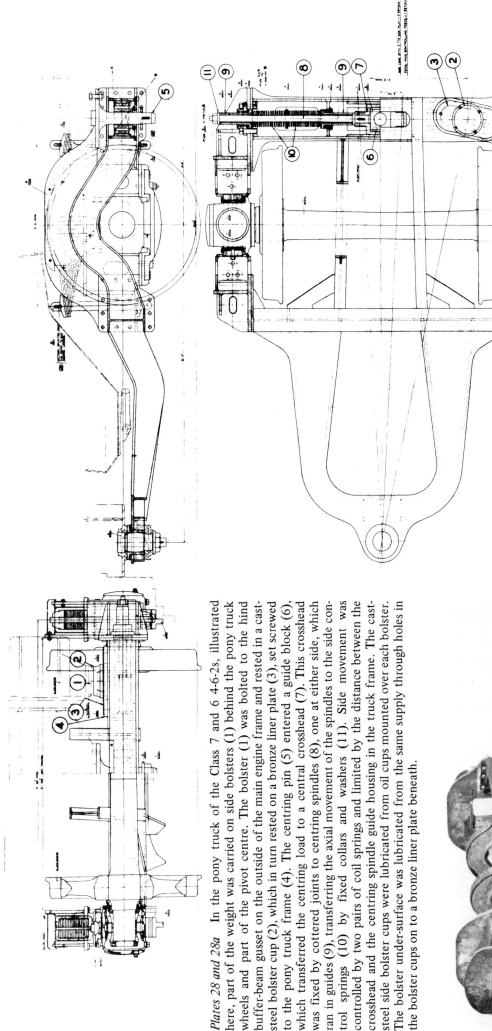

Plates 28 and 28a In the pony truck of the Class 7 and 6 4-6-2s, illustrated here, part of the weight was carried on side bolsters (1) behind the pony truck wheels and part of the pivot centre. The bolster (1) was bolted to the hind buffer-beam gusset on the outside of the main engine frame and rested in a cast-steel bolster cup (2), which in turn rested on a bronze liner plate (3), set screwed to the pony truck frame (4). The centring pin (5) entered a guide block (6), which transferred the centring load to a central crosshead (7). This crosshead was fixed by cottered joints to centring spindles (8), one at either side, which ran in guides (9), transferring the axial movement of the spindles to the side control springs (10) by fixed collars and washers (11). Side movement was controlled by two pairs of coil springs and limited by the distance between the crosshead and the centring spindle guide housing in the truck frame. The cast-steel side bolster cups were lubricated from oil cups mounted over each bolster. The bolster under-surface was lubricated from the same supply through holes in the bolster cups on to a bronze liner plate beneath.

'DUKE OF GLOUCESTER'
Prototype CLASS 8, 4-6-2 Tender Engine No. 71000

Plates 29 to 31 Three views of No. 71000 *Duke of Gloucester* on completion at Crewe Works in May 1954. This engine was regarded as a replacement for Stanier Pacific No. 46202 *Princess Anne*, wrecked in the Harrow disaster of 1952, and was a prototype Standard Class 8 Pacific. The design was based on that of the 'Britannia', but with three cylinders, British Caprotti valve gear and enlarged boiler. Immediately on completion, almost certainly before even being steamed, this engine was sent to Willesden shed for inclusion in the exhibition of BR rolling stock, organised for the International Railway Congress. It was so named because the Duke of Gloucester performed the opening ceremony of the Congress.

BRITISH RAILWAYS STANDARD, CLASS 8, 4-6-2 Tender Engine

BRITISH-CAPROTTI VALVE GEAR

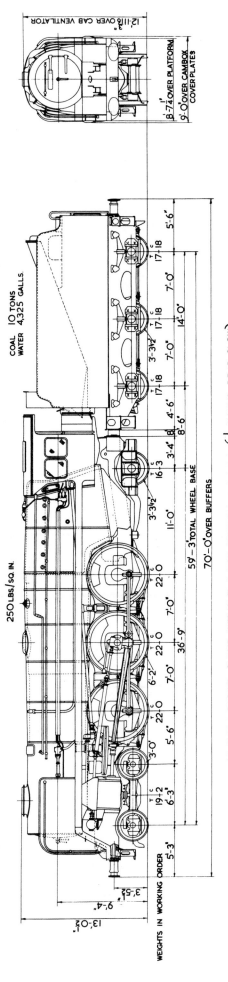

250 LBS/SQ. IN.

		FULL	EMPTY
WEIGHTS		T. C.	T. C.
ENGINE		101-5	92-0
TENDER		53-14	24-8
TOTAL		154-19	116-8

SCALE 0 2 4 6 8 10

		FULL	EMPTY
WEIGHTS		T. C.	T. C.
ENGINE		101-5	92-0
TENDER		55-10	24-8
TOTAL		156-15	116-8

MINIMUM RADIUS CURVE WITHOUT GAUGE WIDENING 6 CHAINS (4½ CHAINS DEAD SLOW)

CYLINDERS (THREE)	18" x 28"	
TRACTIVE EFFORT	39,080 LBS.	
ADHESION FACTOR	3-78	
BRAKE % ENGINE & TENDER	51-17	
BOILER TYPE	B.R. 13	
TENDER TYPE	B.R. 1J.	

BOILER BARREL DIAMETER (OUTSIDE): 5'-9" INCREASING TO 6'-5½"
FIREBOX (OUTSIDE): 8'-0⅛" LONG x 7'-9" TO 7'-4" WIDE
TUBES: 40 LARGE 5⅛"O.D. x 7 S.W.G. / 136 SMALL 2⅛"O.D. x 11 S.W.G.
SUPERHEATER ELEMENTS: 1⅜"O.D. x 9 S.W.G.
LENGTH BETWEEN TUBEPLATES: 17'-0"
HEATING SURFACES: TUBES 2264 SQ. FT.
FIREBOX 226 SQ. FT.
TOTAL EVAPORATIVE 2490 SQ. FT.
SUPERHEATER 677 SQ. FT.
FREE FLUE AREA 6-8 SQ. FT.
GRATE AREA 48-6 SQ. FT.

BOILER TYPE B.P. 13
TENDER TYPE B.R. 1E.

Plate 32 Drawing of No. 71000 with the BR 1J tender fitted in November 1957. The BR 1E tender originally built for this engine was closely similar to the 1D tenders of Nos. 70045-54, except that the weight on the leading axle was 1 ton more at 18 tons 10 cwt, and is illustrated *left*.

Plates 33 and 34 Two views of the frames and cylinders of No. 71000 in the erecting shop at Crewe Works, with the bogie, ashpan, cab floor and trailing truck alongside. The main frames of all the wide firebox engines, the 4-6-2s and 2-10-0s, were designed with the frames positioned centrally above the horn guides, as on Bulleid's 'Merchant Navies', and the spacing of the frames was therefore narrower than normal on British engines. Substantial cross-bracing was provided, for longer frame life, and the rear extension frames beneath the firebox were thick but shallow, to allow for a deep ashpan. The lay-out of the British Caprotti valve gear was designed with great care: the drive for the cam boxes of the outside cylinders was taken off the middle driving wheels by worm gear-boxes mounted on return cranks; the cam box of the inside cylinder, accessibly positioned in front of the smokebox saddle, was driven by an extension from the worm shaft of the left-hand cam box through a right-angle bevel gear. The shaft from the reverser in the cab, on the left-hand side of the engine, operated through reversing gearboxes to the rear of the cylinders.

British Rail

Plate 35 No. 71000 under construction in the erecting shop. The boiler was basically a 'Britannia' boiler with enlarged grate area and double chimney.
British Rail

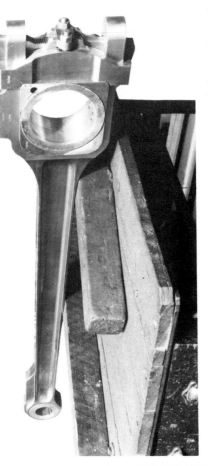

Plate 38 The inside connecting rod of No. 71000, showing the fork-type big end with its robust clip closing the jaws of the rod and the serrated locking device which allowed the correct degree of tightness to be applied and locked. Inside big ends were traditionally a source of trouble but this arrangement, designed by J.F. Harrison, was most successful.
British Rail

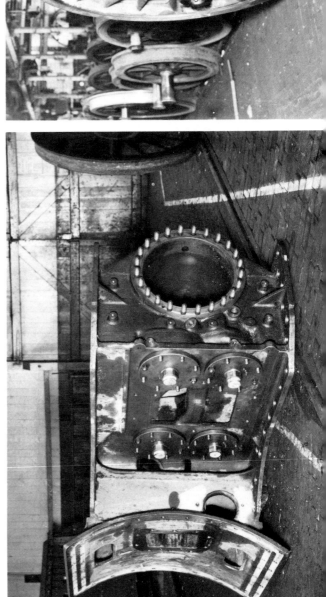

Plate 39 The centre driving wheels and crank axle of No. 71000, the only crank axle fitted to a BR Standard engine.
British Rail

Plates 36 and 37 Two views of the casting for the inside cylinder, which also incorporated the smokebox saddle and slide-bar carriers. Each cylinder had separate inlet and exhaust valves at each end.
British Rail

Plate 40 View of No. 71000 *Duke of Gloucester* taken at Swindon during the period in late 1954 and early 1955 when the engine was transferred there for controlled road testing.

British Rail

Plate 42 No. 71000 *Duke of Gloucester* approaching Stafford with an up express about 1960. It is 'running in' after overhaul at Crewe Works. Now classified 8P, instead of simply 8, it has acquired a single wide footstep under the smokebox, the post-1956 emblem and **AWS** equipment, the battery box for which is located on the running plate just ahead of the firebox. The tender is the **BR 1J** type built for the engine in November 1957.

J. B. Bucknall

Plate 43 Duke of Gloucester at Crewe Works after withdrawal in 1962, awaiting a decision on possible preservation. After some time it was decided that only the cylinders would be preserved but fortunately the engine was later rescued from Barry by a preservation group and is now at Loughborough.

J. B. Bucknall

Plate 41 The rear of the **BR 1E** tender of No. 71000. This tender was basically the same as the 1D tenders of the last batch of 'Britannias' but had a nominal capacity of 10 tons of coal instead of 9 tons; it had the same water capacity, 4,725 gallons, and the same type of coal pusher. After experience with No. 71000 in service, it was decided that greater coal capacity was needed and a new tender designated type BR 1J was built in November 1957. It held more coal, though still nominally only 10 tons, and less water, 4,325 gallons, and is easily distinguished in photographs, as the curved top over the sides of the coal space extended further to the rear than on the 1E type, with a much-reduced rear 'cut-away'. In an official list of drawings the water capacity is given as 4,425 gallons, but most sources give 4,325 gallons.

British Rail

'CLAN'
CLASS 6, 4-6-2 Tender Engines
Nos. 72000 ~ 72009

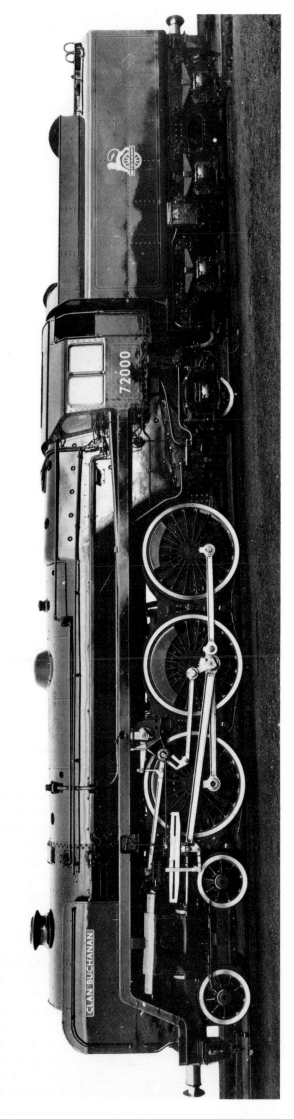

Plate 44   The first of the 'Clan' Class 6 4-6-2s, No. 72000 *Clan Buchanan*, at Crewe Works on completion in December 1951. Basically, these engines had the 'Britannia' chassis with a smaller boiler, and so had a route availability comparable to the Class 5 4-6-0s. They were designed for Class 6 and the harder Class 5 duties. Though originally intended for the Highland main line from Perth to Inverness, the whole class was allocated to Carlisle Kingmoor and Polmadie sheds.

British Rail

BRITISH RAILWAYS STANDARD, CLASS 6, 4-6-2 Tender Engine

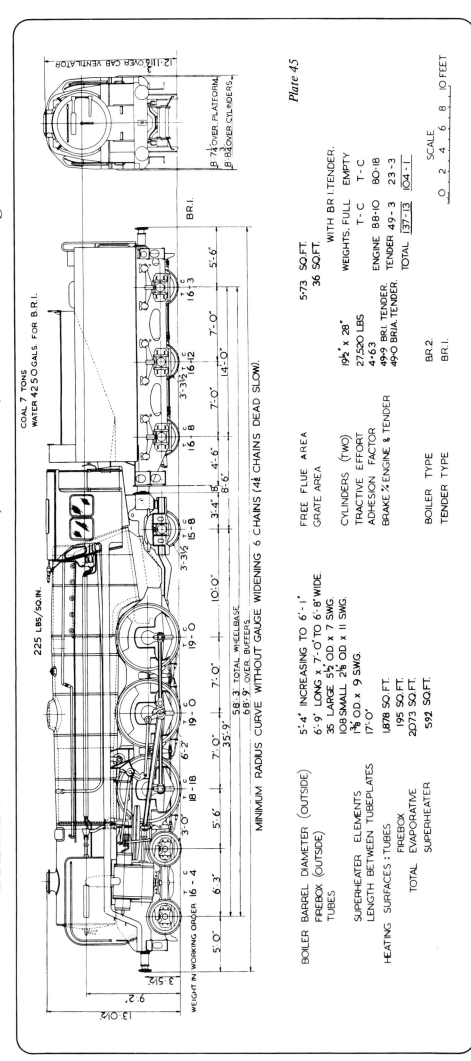

12-11⅛ OVER CAB VENTILATOR

8-7¼ OVER PLATFORM
8-8¼ OVER CYLINDERS

COAL 7 TONS
WATER 4 2 5 0 GALS. FOR B.R.I.

225 LBS/SQ.IN.

Plate 45

WEIGHT IN WORKING ORDER

13-0½"
9-2"
3-5½"

5'-0"   6'-3"   7'-0"   5'-6"   3'-0"   8'-6"   4'-6"   7'-0"   7'-0"   5'-6"
T·C   T·C   T·C   T·C   8'-8"   T·C   T·C   T·C   T·C
16-4   18-18   19-0 19-0 3-3½   15-8   16-8   16-12   16-3
                                      6-2   3-3½   14'-0"

35-9"
58-3 TOTAL WHEELBASE
68-9 OVER BUFFERS

MINIMUM RADIUS CURVE WITHOUT GAUGE WIDENING 6 CHAINS (4½ CHAINS DEAD SLOW).

BR.I.

BOILER BARREL DIAMETER (OUTSIDE)	5'-4" INCREASING TO 6'-1"
FIREBOX (OUTSIDE)	6'-9" LONG x 7'-0" TO 6'-8" WIDE.
TUBES	35 LARGE 5½ OD. x 7 SWG.
	108 SMALL 2⅛ OD. x 11 SWG.
SUPERHEATER ELEMENTS	1⅜ OD. x 9 SWG.
LENGTH BETWEEN TUBEPLATES	17'-0"
HEATING SURFACES : TUBES	1,878 SQ.FT.
FIREBOX	195 SQ.FT.
TOTAL EVAPORATIVE	2073 SQ.FT.
SUPERHEATER	592 SQ.FT.

FREE FLUE AREA	5·73 SQ.FT.	
GRATE AREA	36 SQ.FT.	
		WITH BR I.TENDER.
		WEIGHTS. FULL EMPTY
CYLINDERS (TWO)	19½" x 28"	T-C T-C
TRACTIVE EFFORT	27,520 LBS	
ADHESION FACTOR	4·63	ENGINE 88-10 80-18
BRAKE % ENGINE & TENDER	49·9 BR.I. TENDER.	TENDER 49-3 23-3
	49·0 BRIA. TENDER.	TOTAL 137-13 104 - 1
BOILER TYPE	BR.2.	
TENDER TYPE	BR.I.	

SCALE
0   2   4   6   8   10 FEET

Plate 46 No. 72008 *Clan MacLeod* under the wires at Crewe in the early 1960s while working a football special from Carlisle to Coventry.

J. H. Hardy

Plate 47 (below) No. 72006, formerly named *Clan Mackenzie* but without nameplates, at Carlisle Kingmoor shed in the last days of BR steam. This engine was the last 'Clan' to be withdrawn, in May 1966. The fitting of AWS (shown by the cylinder beneath the cab), the speedometer (driven off the rear driving wheel), and the LMS-type mounting of the return crank, on four studs instead of a square pin, are the main alterations from the condition as built. The yellow stripe on the cabside was applied to the engine in error. From 1st September, 1964, certain classes, mainly of LMS origin, were prohibited from working over electrified lines south of Crewe and had yellow stripes applied to denote this. BR Standard classes, however, were not affected by the ban.

Author

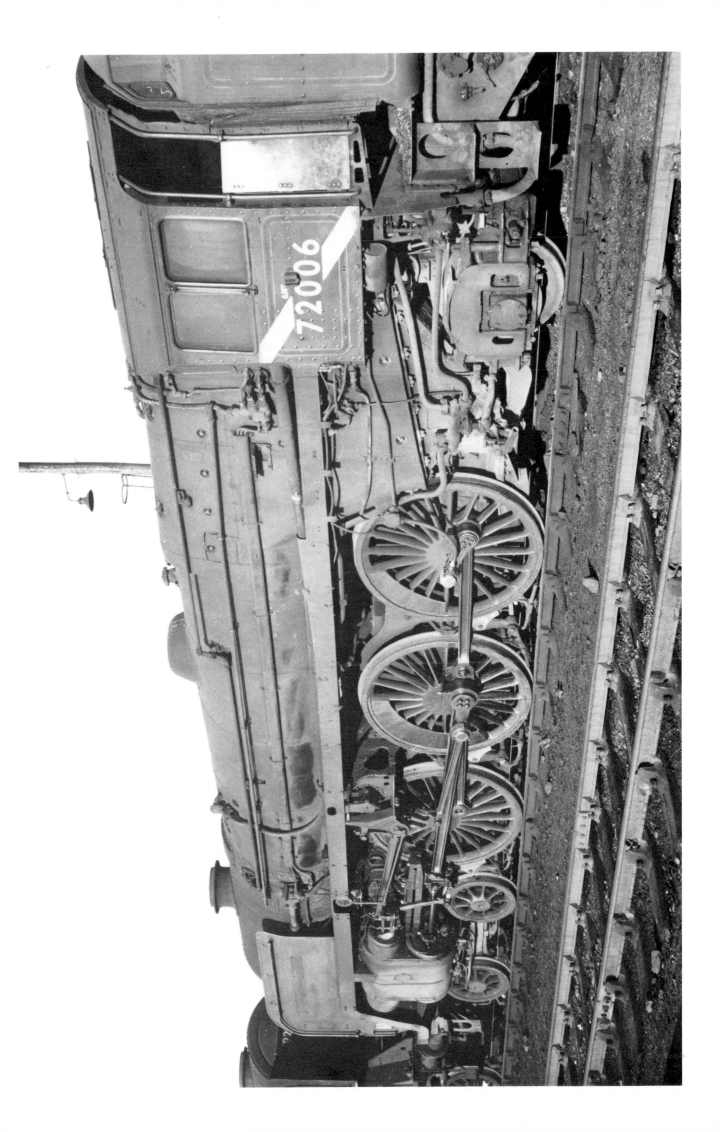

Plate 49 No. 72002 *Clan Campbell* at Polmadie shed, Glasgow, on 12th April, 1952.

Plate 48 The last 'Clan' No. 72009 *Clan Stewart*, on completion at Crewe Works in April 1952. After the first batch of only ten engines, no further 'Clans' were built. Fifteen more were included in the 1952 building programme, five for the Southern Region and ten more for the Scottish, but the order was cancelled. *British Rail*

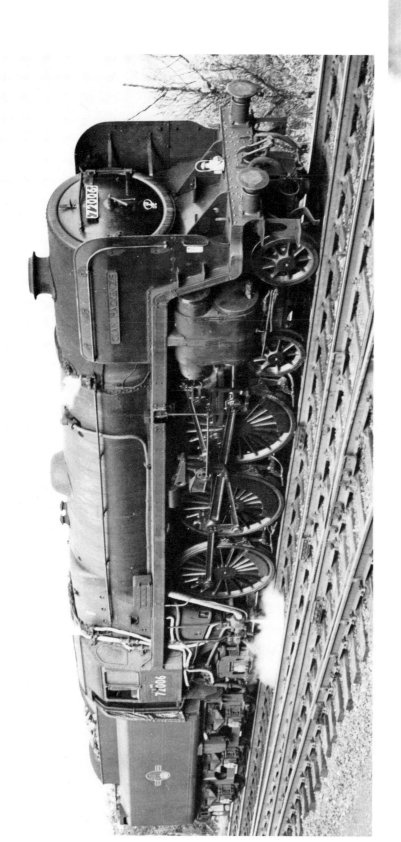

Plate 50 No. 72006 *Clan Mackenzie* standing at Greskine signal box, half way down Beattock bank, on 11th October, 1963. The AWS battery box is located on the running plate just ahead of the firebox.

Hugh Ballantyne

Plate 51 No. 72008 *Clan Macleod* passing Hilton Junction, Perth, in June 1964 with an up parcels train. It is in the sadly neglected condition which was all too common in the latter years of BR steam, covered in grime and without nameplates.

Author

CLASS 5, 4-6-0 Tender Engines
Nos. 73000 ~ 73154

Plate 52 The first of the Standard Class 5 4-6-0s, No. 73000, at Derby on completion in April 1951. Its mixed-traffic livery of glossy black lined in the LNWR style was quickly changed in one slight detail. The red line round the inner edges of the side of the running plate, in the same manner as the orange line on the standard green livery of the Pacifics, was replaced by lining of red, cream and grey along the lower edge only. Some accounts say that there was a single red line along the lower edge only but this photograph clearly shows otherwise.

British Rail

BRITISH RAILWAYS STANDARD, *CLASS 5, 4-6-0 Tender Engine*

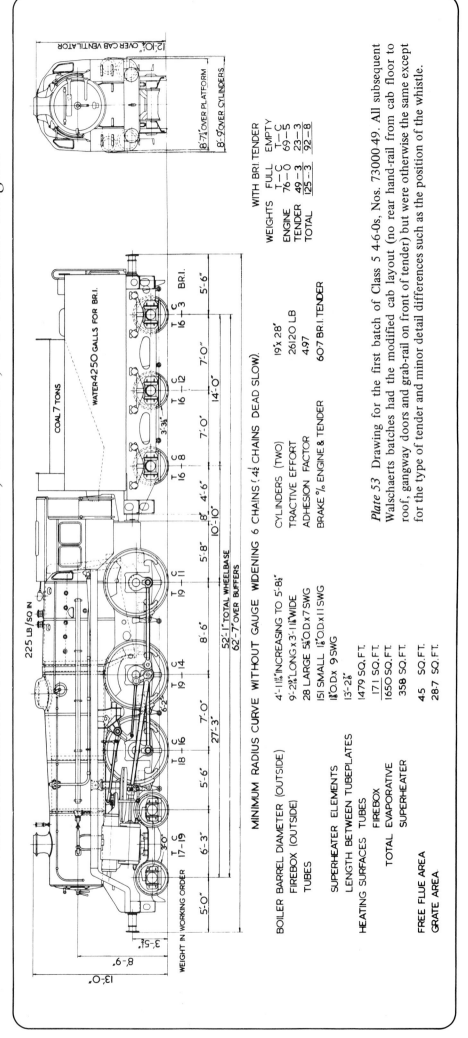

225 LB/SQ IN

COAL 7 TONS

WATER 4250 GALLS FOR BR.I.

12'-10½" OVER CAB VENTILATOR

8'-7¼" OVER PLATFORM
8'-9" OVER CYLINDERS

WEIGHT IN WORKING ORDER

| 5'-0" | 6'-3" | 7'-0" | 5'-6" | 8'-6" | 7'-0" | 5'-8" | 8' | 4'-6" | 7'-0" | 7'-0" | 5'-6" |

T C 17-19 T C 18-16 T C 19-14 T C 19-11 T C 16-8 T C 16-12 T C 16-3 BR.I.

10'-10"   14'-0"

27'-3"

52'-1" TOTAL WHEELBASE

62'-7" OVER BUFFERS

3'-0" 6'-2" 3'-3½"

3'-5½"

8'-9"

13'-0"

MINIMUM RADIUS CURVE WITHOUT GAUGE WIDENING 6 CHAINS (4½ CHAINS DEAD SLOW).

BOILER BARREL DIAMETER (OUTSIDE)	4'-11⅝" INCREASING TO 5'-8½"
FIREBOX (OUTSIDE)	9'-2¹³⁄₁₆" LONG x 3'-1⅛" WIDE
TUBES	28 LARGE 5⅛" OD x 7 SWG
	151 SMALL 1⅞" OD x 11 SWG
SUPERHEATER ELEMENTS	1⅜" O.D. x 9 SWG
LENGTH BETWEEN TUBEPLATES	13'-2⅜"
HEATING SURFACES TUBES	1479 SQ.FT.
FIREBOX	171 SQ.FT.
TOTAL EVAPORATIVE	1650 SQ.FT.
SUPERHEATER	358 SQ.FT.
FREE FLUE AREA	4·5 SQ.FT.
GRATE AREA	28·7 SQ.FT.

CYLINDERS (TWO)	19 x 28'
TRACTIVE EFFORT	26120 LB
ADHESION FACTOR	4·97
BRAKE % ENGINE & TENDER	60·7 BR.I. TENDER

WITH BR.I. TENDER

WEIGHTS	FULL	EMPTY
	T - C	T - C
ENGINE	76 - 0	69 - 5
TENDER	49 - 3	23 - 3
TOTAL	125 - 3	92 - 8

Plate 53 Drawing for the first batch of Class 5 4-6-0s, Nos. 73000-49. All subsequent Walschaerts batches had the modified cab layout (no rear hand-rail from cab floor to roof, gangway doors and grab-rail on front of tender) but were otherwise the same except for the type of tender and minor detail differences such as the position of the whistle.

Plate 54 The second five of the first batch were allocated to the Scottish Region and were beautifully kept in the traditional manner of front-line engines in Scotland. Here, No. 73008 awaits the right-away from Perth with the up 'Saint Mungo' on 3rd September, 1955. The cylinder and piston ends, buffers, coupling, frame edges, smokebox handles and handrails are all burnished, and the backgrounds of the numberplate and shed plate have been repainted probably in light blue (although sometimes maroon was used for this).

A. G. Ellis Collection

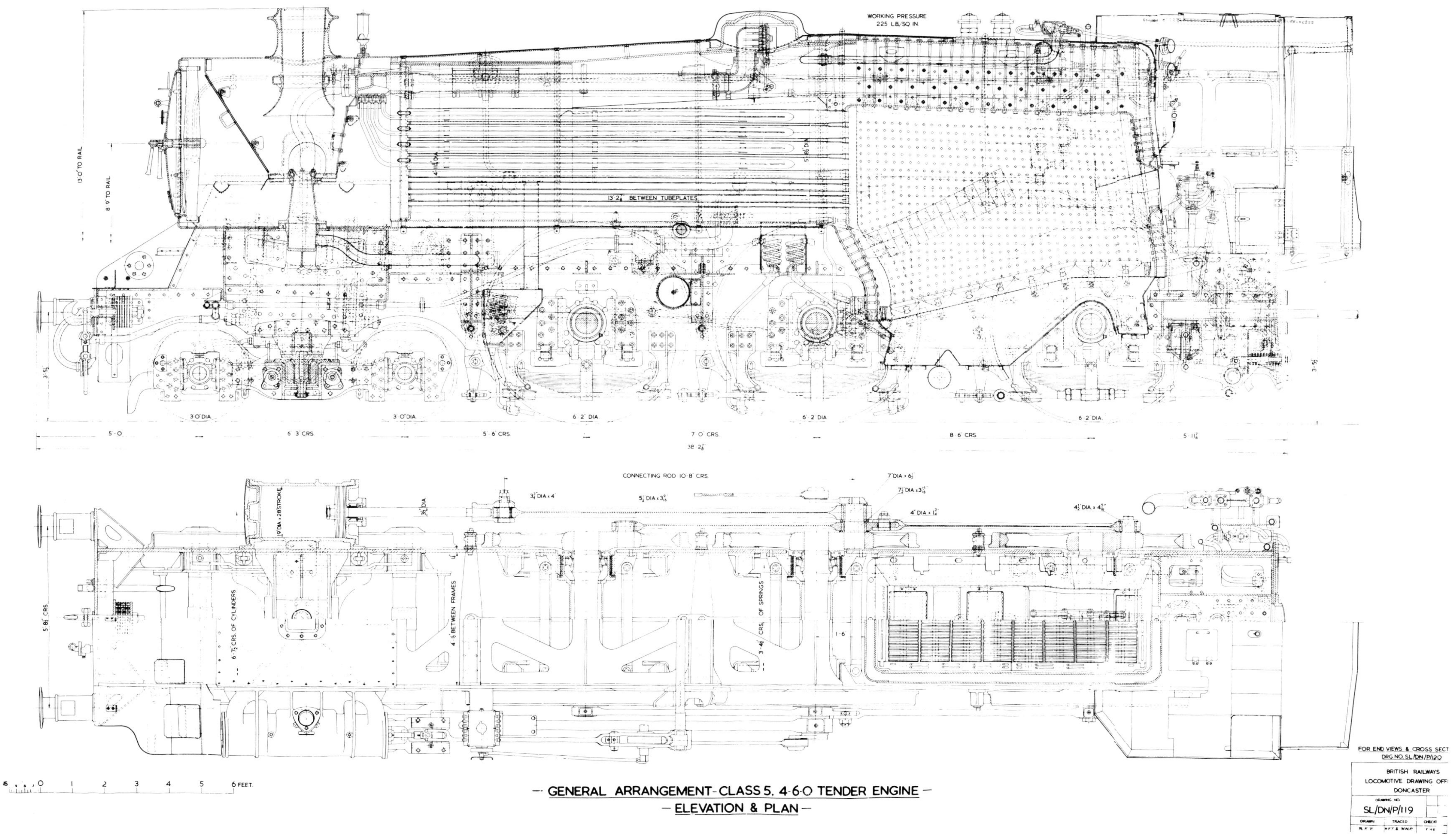

WORKING PRESSURE
225 LB/SQ IN
13'-0" TO RAIL
8'-9" TO RAIL
13'-2⅞" BETWEEN TUBEPLATES
3'-0" DIA
6'-2" DIA
5'-0
6'-3" CRS
5'-6" CRS
7'-0" CRS
8'-6" CRS
5'-11⅞"
38'-2⅞"
CONNECTING ROD 10'-8" CRS
7" DIA x 6½"
4¼" DIA x 4⅝"
19" DIA x 28" STROKE
6'-7½" CRS OF CYLINDERS
4'-1½" BETWEEN FRAMES
3'-4½" CRS. OF SPRINGS
5'-8½" CRS
0 1 2 3 4 5 6 FEET
FOR END VIEWS & CROSS SECT
DRG NO. SL/DN/P/120
BRITISH RAILWAYS
LOCOMOTIVE DRAWING OFF
DONCASTER
SL/DN/P/119

— GENERAL ARRANGEMENT - CLASS 5, 4-6-0 TENDER ENGINE —

— ELEVATION & PLAN —

Plate 55

Plate 56 The front of the **BR** 1 tender fitted to No. 73023, after some years in service. It has been modified with screens and rubber flaps to combat draughts. On the left of the tender is the handle for working the scoop and beside it is the water gauge and above it the locker for the crew's belongings. On the other side is the hand brake and above it the tunnel for the fire-irons. No fall-plate was fitted on the original BR tenders and gangway doors were carried on the rear of the engine cabs.

British Rail

Plate 57 The second of the Standard Class 5s, No. 73001, in the livery which was applied to all the **BR** Standard tender engines, except the Pacific and 9F 2-10-0s, and to all the tank engines. Many major parts were the same as on the 'Britannias' and 'Clans', the bogie and **BR** 1 tender, for example, as were many minor features which were later changed, such as the fluted coupling rods and the lubricator hidden behind the side of the running plate, which was soon cut away for accessibility. The Class 5s were the smallest Standard engines to have three-tone chime whistles, mounted behind the chimney and operated by a cable running from the cab down the right-hand boiler handrail.

British Rail

Plate 58 From November 1956 Swindon began to apply lined green livery both to ex-GWR classes and to BR Standard classes which had hitherto been black. This view shows Class 5 4-6-0 No. 73035 at Swindon in 1957 after repainting in the new green livery. It differs slightly from that of the Pacifics in that there is only a single yellow line along the lower edge of the running plate, in the same fashion as the lined black livery, whereas the Pacifics had an orange line around the inner edges of the running plate to form a panel. The plating is now cut away over the lubricator, WR lamp irons are fitted, as is a speedometer, but there are no draught screens, just flaps from the tender on to the rear of the cab floor. *British Rail*

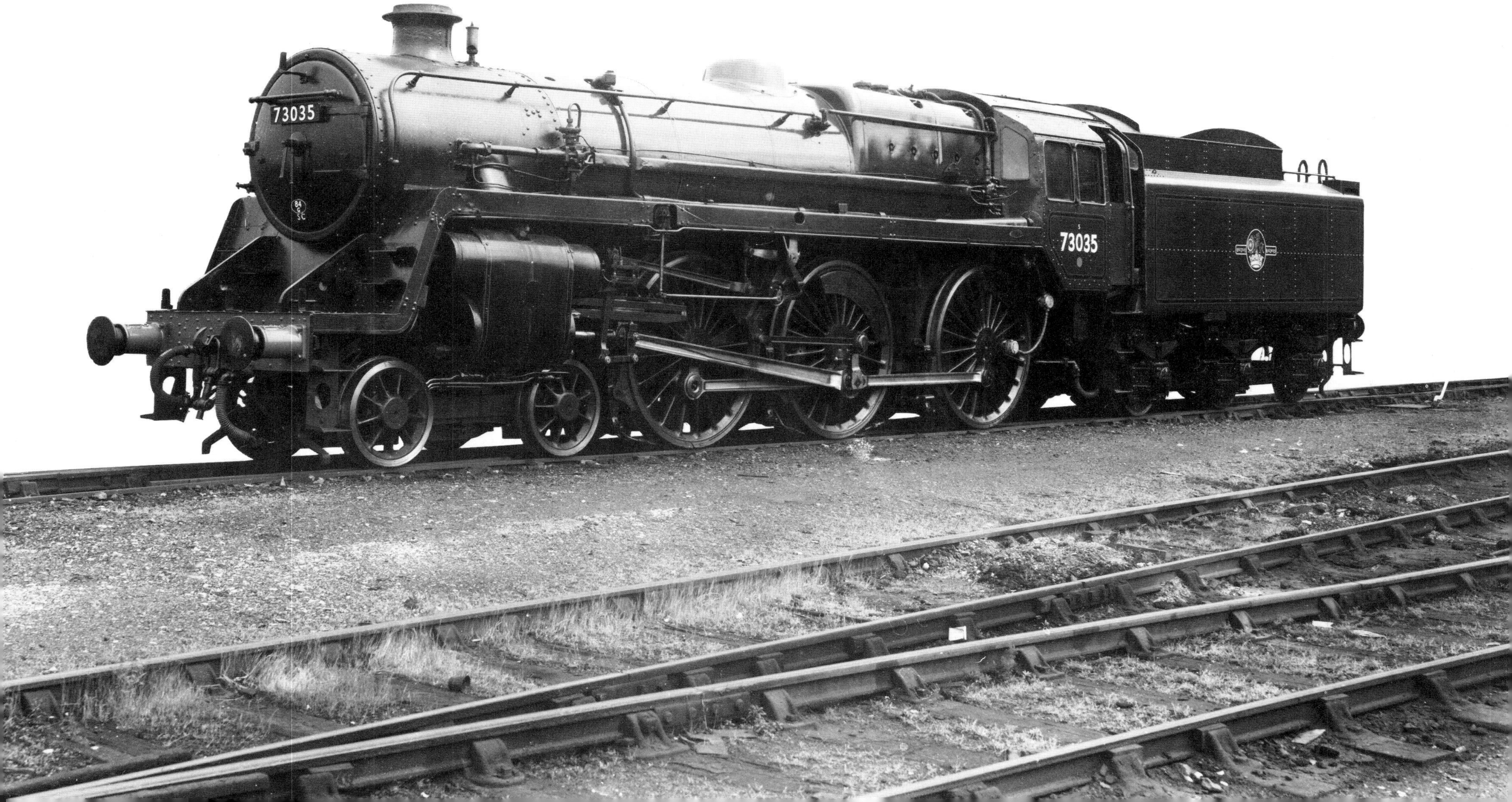

Plate 59 No. 73054, built in June 1954, at Bath Junction with the 12.00 from Templecombe to Bath on 11th March, 1964. It is in green livery but as on the Pacifics there is orange lining round the inner edges of the running plate. This was standard Eastleigh practice for all engines painted green there, the variation in the photograph of No. 73035 appearing only on Swindon repaints. The coupling rods are rectangular section, introduced on this class with No. 73050, and there is a horizontal footstep on the rear of the tender to enable the fireman to stand there when filling the tank.

Hugh Ballantyne

Plate 62 The cab of No. 73133, in the erecting shop at Derby Works in 1957. This view clearly shows the re-design of the cab rear to avoid the draughts of the original arrangement. The extended floor is retained but now fits under a short but full-width fall-plate on the front of the tender, which also carries the gangway doors.

British Rail

Plate 60 No. 73030 at Crewe North shed on 28th November, 1954. Like the two 'Britannias', Nos. 70043-4, two Class 5 4-6-0s, Nos. 73030-1, were fitted from new with air-brake equipment, which was removed after completion of trials with air-braked freight trains.

T.J. Edgington

Plate 61 No. 73089 *Maid of Astolat*, one of the twenty Southern Region Standard Class 5s which were given the names formerly carried by the Urie 'King Arthurs' in 1959-60.

J.H. Russell

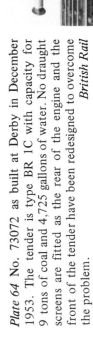

Plate 63 A rear view of a **BR** 1C tender as No. 73073 takes water at Leicester. The water column was a new type introduced in the mid-1950s and designed to be operated from ground level, so as to avoid the need for the heavy leather bag to be manhandled into the tender.

British Rail

Plate 64 No. 73072 as built at Derby in December 1953. The tender is type BR 1C with capacity for 9 tons of coal and 4,725 gallons of water. No draught screens are fitted as the rear of the engine and the front of the tender have been redesigned to overcome the problem.

British Rail

BRITISH RAILWAYS STANDARD, *CLASS 5, 4-6-0 Tender Engine*

BRITISH-CAPROTTI VALVE GEAR

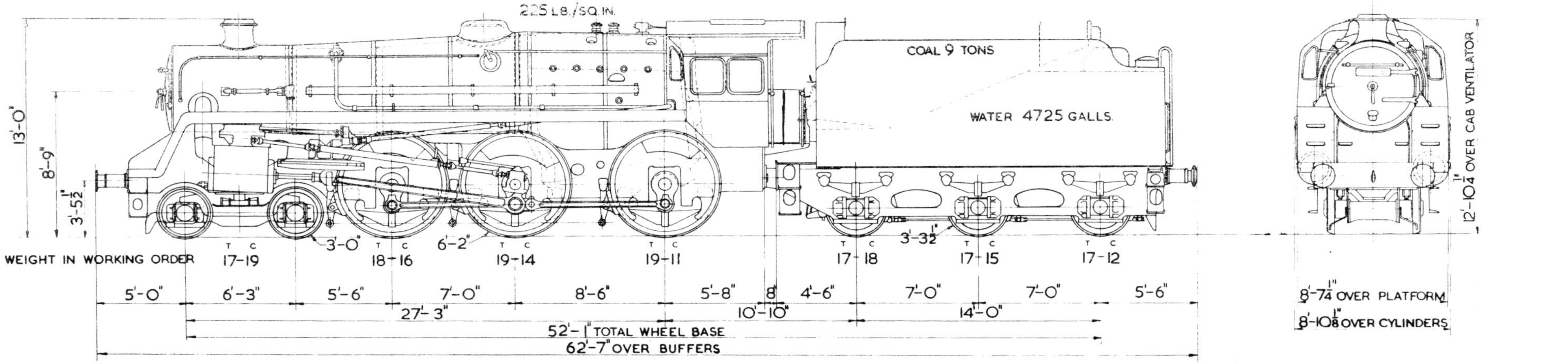

225 LB./SQ.IN.
COAL 9 TONS
WATER 4725 GALLS.
13'-0"
8'-9"
3'-5 1/2"
3'-0"
6'-2"
3'-3 1/2"
WEIGHT IN WORKING ORDER
T C 17-19
T C 18-16
T C 19-14
T C 19-11
T C 17-18
T C 17-15
T C 17-12
5'-0"
6'-3"
5'-6"
7'-0"
8'-6"
5'-8"
8"
4'-6"
7'-0"
7'-0"
5'-6"
27'-3"
10'-10"
14'-0"
52'-1" TOTAL WHEEL BASE
62'-7" OVER BUFFERS
12'-10 1/4" OVER CAB VENTILATOR
8'-7 1/4" OVER PLATFORM
8'-10 1/8" OVER CYLINDERS

MINIMUM RADIUS CURVE WITHOUT GAUGE WIDENING 6 CHAINS (4½ CHAINS DEAD SLOW)

BOILER BARREL DIAMETER (OUTSIDE)	4'-11 11/16" INCREASING TO 5'-8 1/2"
FIREBOX (OUTSIDE)	9'-2 13/16" LONG x 3'-11 7/8" WIDE
TUBES	28 LARGE 5 1/8" O.D. x 7 S.W.G. 151 SMALL 1 7/8" O.D. x 11 S.W.G.
SUPERHEATER ELEMENTS	1 3/8" O.D. x 9 S.W.G.
LENGTH BETWEEN TUBEPLATES	13'-2 7/8"
HEATING SURFACES: TUBES	1479 SQ. FT.
FIREBOX	171 SQ. FT.
TOTAL EVAPORATIVE	1650 SQ. FT.
SUPERHEATER	358 SQ. FT.
FREE FLUE AREA	4·5 SQ. FT.
GRATE AREA	28·7 SQ. FT.

CYLINDERS (TWO)	19" x 28"
TRACTIVE EFFORT	26 120 LBS.
ADHESION FACTOR	4·97
BRAKE % ENGINE & TENDER	61·5
BOILER TYPE	B.R. 3.
TENDER TYPE	B.R. 1 C.

WEIGHTS	FULL	EMPTY
	T. C.	T. C.
ENGINE	76-0	69-5
TENDER	53-5	23-3
TOTAL	129-5	92-8

SCALE 0 2 4 6 8 10 FEET

Plate 65 Drawing for the second batch of Caprotti Class 5 4-6-0s, Nos. 73135-44 (the other batches differed only in the type of tender). The Caprottis were identical to the Walschaerts Class 5s from No. 73050 onwards, in having gangway doors and a grab-rail on the tender.

Plate 66 As the British Caprotti valve gear on No. 71000 had proved so successful, a batch of thirty Class 5s, Nos. 73125-54, was similarly equipped. They were built at Derby in 1956-7 and allocated ten each to the Western, London Midland and Scottish Regions.

Here, No. 73125 is seen ex-works at Derby in a view which clearly shows the unusual arrangement of the partitions in the BR 1B tender. From No. 73100 onwards the practice of mounting a chime whistle behind the chimney ceased and instead an ordinary whistle was fitted on top of the firebox. Another minor modification was that the front windows in the cab were hinged instead of fixed.

British Rail

Plates 67 and 68 Two views of the Caprotti valve gear on the right-hand side of No. 73133.

British Rail

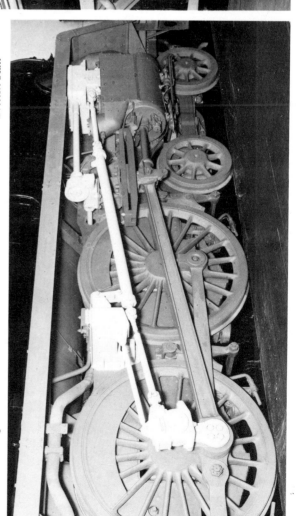

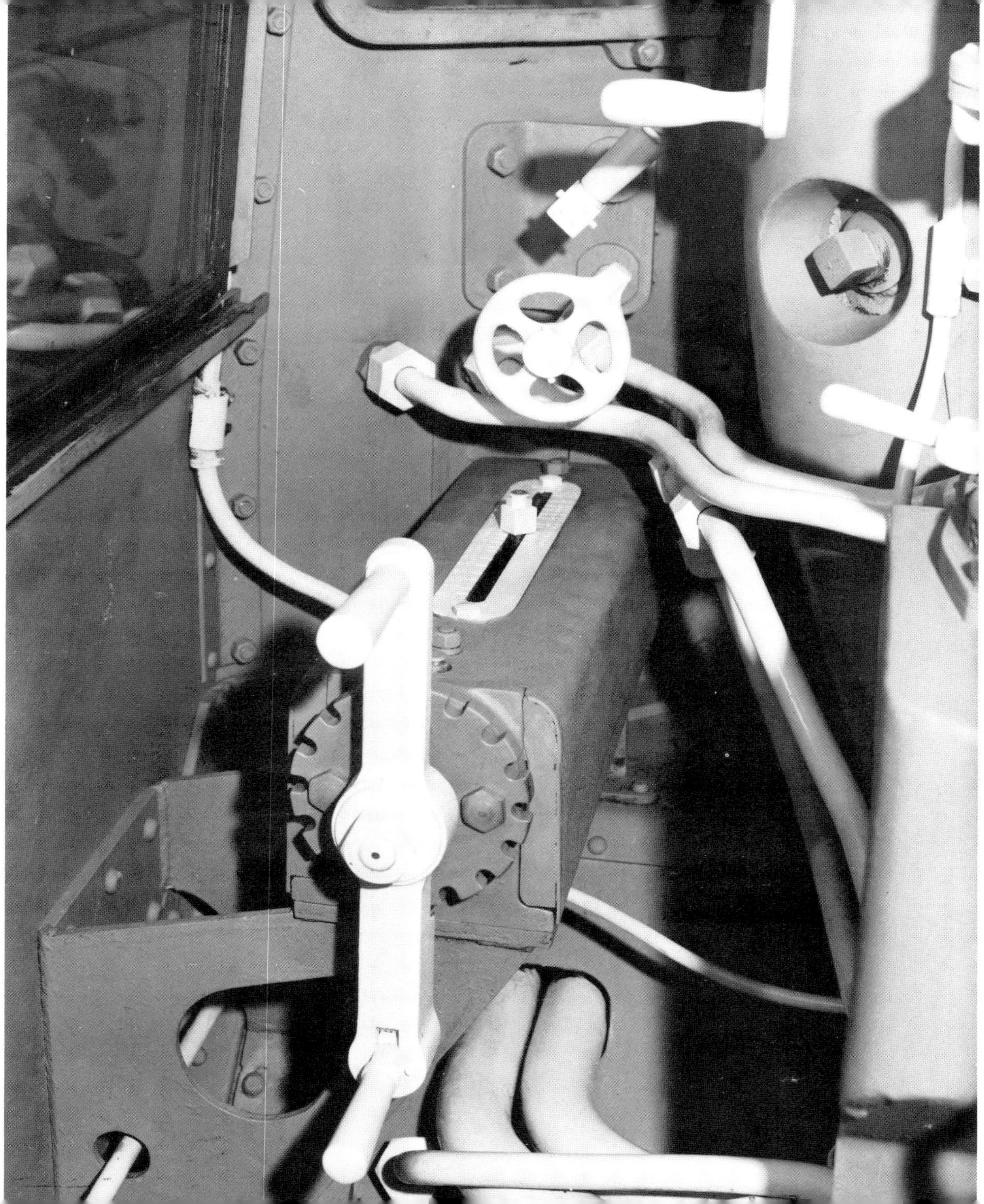

Plate 69 A close-up of the reverser on No. 73133, showing the reversing wheel end-on to the tubular reversing shaft. Early BR Standards had the 'mangle-wheel' reverser, positioned at right angles to the shaft and driving it through bevel gears. Consequently, it was often stiff and difficult to operate.

British Rail

Plate 70 Driver R. Evry, then the most senior driver in the top link at Bath, at the controls of No. 73047, bringing the 09.03 from Bristol to Bournemouth West into Templecombe on 13th July, 1963.

Hugh Ballantyne

Plate 71 The last of the Caprotti fitted Class 5s, No. 73154, on completion at Derby Works in 1957.

British Rail

Plate 72   No. 73132 ex works at Darlington on 10th October, 1964. The lining on the running plate has either been omitted or is still to be applied. Because the Caprotti valve gear could not provide reciprocating motion to operate the mechanical lubricators, which were positioned one on either side of the Walschaerts engines, both lubricators were positioned on the right-hand side of the Caprottis and driven off the rear driving wheel (as on the LMS Caprotti 5s). In turn, this required the relocation of the various pipes normally hidden under the footplating, the most prominent of which is that delivering exhaust steam to the exhaust steam injector. In this picture a piece of string is tied from the handrail to the spindle of one of the lubricators.

G. W. Morrison

Plate 73 A rear view of No. 73133 receiving attention at Patricroft on 20th December, 1965.

L. A. Nixon

Plate 74 No. 73111, a Doncaster-built engine allocated to the Southern Region. It has the large numerals used by Doncaster for all the Standard engines built there except the Class 4 2-6-0s, and the positioning of the lining on the tender and cab-side also differs by comparison with Derby-built engines.

CLASS 4, 4-6-0 Tender Engines
Nos. 75000 ~ 75079

Plate 75 The first of the Class 4 4-6-0s, No. 75000, photographed on completion at Swindon Works in 1951. It is painted in the mixed-traffic lined black livery. *British Rail*

BRITISH RAILWAYS STANDARD, *CLASS 4, 4-6-0 Tender Engine*

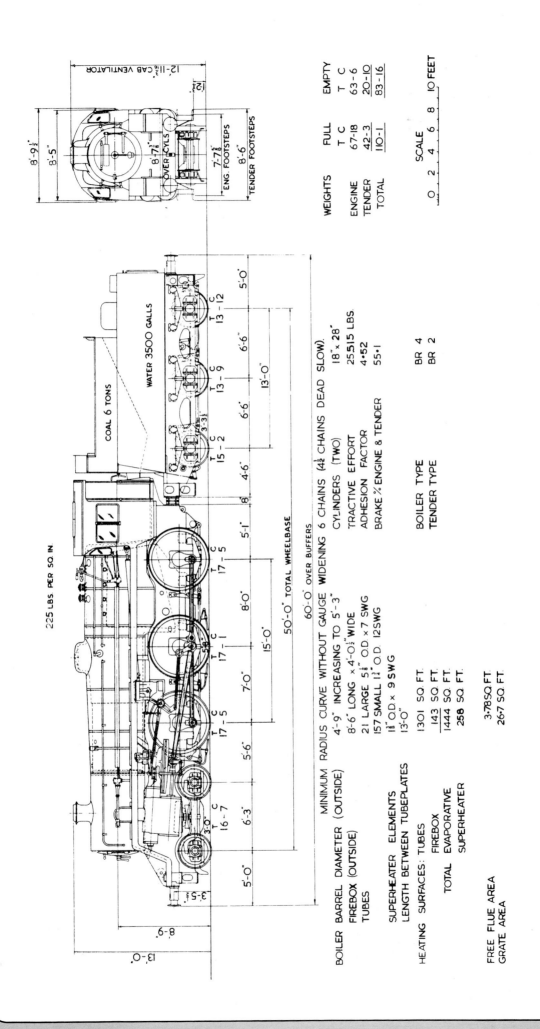

225 LBS PER SQ. IN.

		FULL	EMPTY
WEIGHTS		T C	T C
ENGINE		67-18	63-6
TENDER		42-3	20-10
TOTAL		110-1	83-16

SCALE

0 2 4 6 8 10 FEET

MINIMUM RADIUS CURVE WITHOUT GAUGE WIDENING 6 CHAINS (4½ CHAINS DEAD SLOW).

BOILER BARREL DIAMETER (OUTSIDE)	4'-9" INCREASING TO 5'-3"	CYLINDERS (TWO) 18" × 28"
FIREBOX (OUTSIDE)	8'-6" LONG × 4'-0½" WIDE	TRACTIVE EFFORT 25,515 LBS.
TUBES	21 LARGE 5⅛" O.D. ×7 SWG	ADHESION FACTOR 4·52
	157 SMALL 1¾" O.D. 12SWG	BRAKE % ENGINE & TENDER 55·1
SUPERHEATER ELEMENTS	1⅛" O.D.× 9 SWG	
LENGTH BETWEEN TUBEPLATES	13'-0"	
HEATING SURFACES: TUBES	1301 SQ. FT.	BOILER TYPE BR 4
FIREBOX	143 SQ. FT.	TENDER TYPE BR 2
TOTAL EVAPORATIVE	1444 SQ. FT.	
SUPERHEATER	258 SQ. FT.	
FREE FLUE AREA	3·78 SQ FT	
GRATE AREA	26·7 SQ FT	

Plate 76 Drawing for Class 4 4-6-0s Nos. 75000-49.

Plate 77 No. 75006 on a controlled road test on the Western Region soon after completion. *British Rail*

Plate 78 (below) Rear of the **BR 2** tender of No. 75000. Horizontal footsteps or platforms were later fitted on top of the tank at both sides to make it easier for the fireman to stand there when filling the tank. *British Rail*

Plate 79 (below) View of the cab of No. 75000 as built. The 'mangle-wheel' reverser, fitted to all the original designs, can be clearly seen on the left-hand side in front of the driver's seat. To the right of the seat is the Automatic Train Control apparatus. All BR Standards allocated to the Western Region were naturally fitted with this equipment. The design of the rear of the cab was basically the same on all the first Standard classes. To make things easier for the fireman, who on the conventional British engine had to keep his balance on the cab floor and front of the tender, both moving independently of each other, the cab floor was extended to the rear, so as to come beneath the shovelling plate and no fallplate was fitted. Hand-rails extended from the rear corners of the footplate to the cab roof and gangway doors were fitted to the engine only. Unfortunately, the whole design allowed draughts to rush into the cab from the sides and underneath of the engine.
British Rail

Plate 80 No. 75012 at Llandudno Junction in the mid-1950s. The main modification from the original condition is the fitting of draught screens between engine and tender.
J. B. Bucknall

▼ *Plate 81* No. 75024 in the late 1950s with all the usual modifications: rectangular-section coupling rods, speedometer, draught screens and footstep on the rear of the tender. It is in the green livery used extensively by Swindon at this period, with a single orange line along the lower edge of the running plate.
British Rail

Plate 82 In June 1957 No. 75029 was experimentally fitted with double blast-pipes and chimney and is seen here on conversion, painted in the Swindon green livery. Once the success of the modification had been proved, it was announced that the whole class would be similarly converted but in fact this was never done. The Southern Region allocation was converted at Eastleigh in 1960-1 but the only other members of the class to be so fitted were a handful of the Western Region ones.

British Rail

Plate 83 No. 75074 at Eastleigh shed after overhaul in the works. It has the Brighton design of double chimney and a type BR 1B tender with Timken roller-bearing axleboxes painted yellow with a horizontal red stripe.

J.B. Bucknall

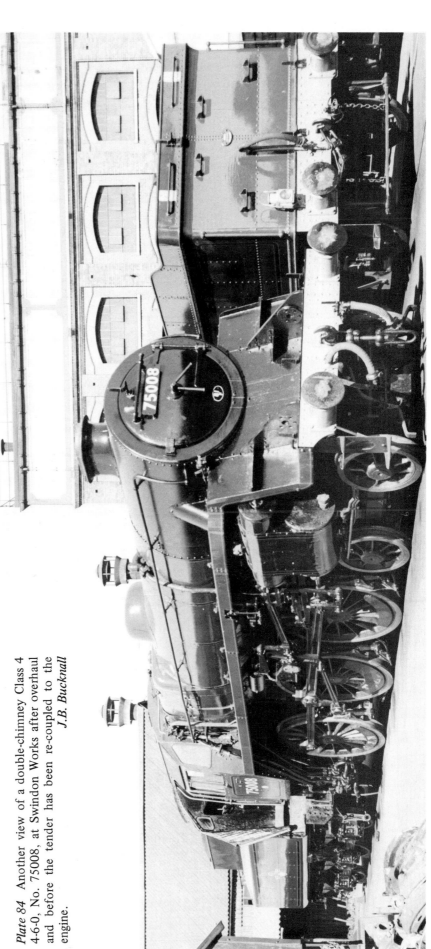

Plate 84 Another view of a double-chimney Class 4 4-6-0, No. 75008, at Swindon Works after overhaul and before the tender has been re-coupled to the engine.

J.B. Bucknall

BRITISH RAILWAYS STANDARD, CLASS 4, 4-6-0 Tender Engine

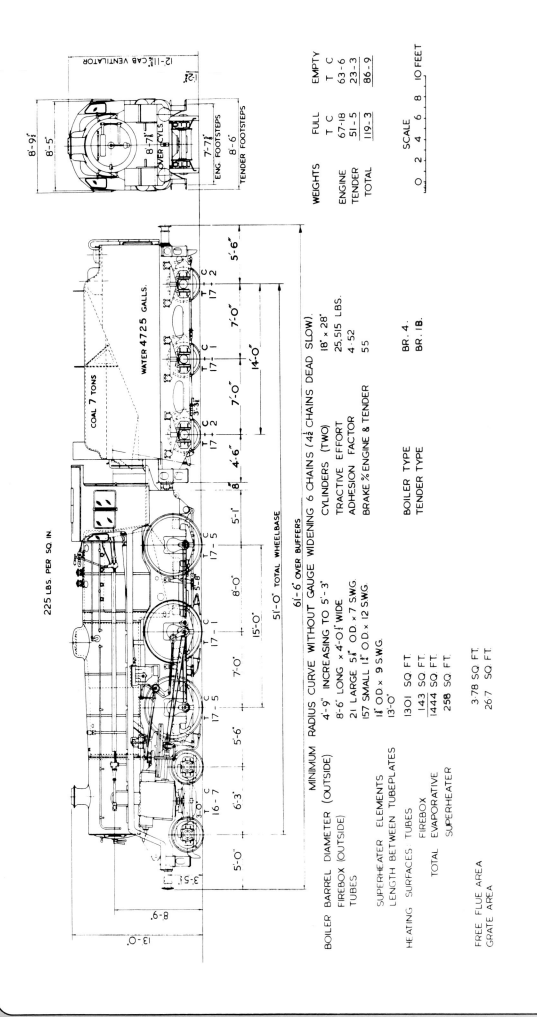

225 LBS. PER SQ IN.

12-11½" CAB VENTILATOR

WATER 4725 GALLS.

COAL 7 TONS

	FULL	EMPTY
WEIGHTS	T C	T C
ENGINE	67-18	63-6
TENDER	51-5	23-3
TOTAL	119-3	86-9

SCALE

O 2 4 6 8 10 FEET

MINIMUM RADIUS CURVE WITHOUT GAUGE WIDENING 6 CHAINS (4½ CHAINS DEAD SLOW).

BOILER BARREL DIAMETER (OUTSIDE)	4'-9" INCREASING TO 5'-3"	CYLINDERS (TWO) 18" × 28"
FIREBOX (OUTSIDE)	8'-6" LONG × 4'-0¼" WIDE	TRACTIVE EFFORT 25,515 LBS.
TUBES	21 LARGE 5¼" O.D. × 7 S.W.G.	ADHESION FACTOR 4·52
	157 SMALL 1" O.D. × 12 S.W.G.	BRAKE % ENGINE & TENDER 55
SUPERHEATER ELEMENTS	11⅜" O.D. × 9 S.W.G.	
LENGTH BETWEEN TUBEPLATES	13'-0"	
		BOILER TYPE BR. 4.
HEATING SURFACES. TUBES	1301 SQ FT.	TENDER TYPE BR. 1B.
FIREBOX	143 SQ FT.	
TOTAL EVAPORATIVE	1444 SQ FT.	
SUPERHEATER	258 SQ FT.	
FREE FLUE AREA	3·78 SQ FT.	
GRATE AREA	26·7 SQ FT	

Plate 85 Drawing for Nos. 75065-79. Nos. 75050-64 had the same arrangement of the rear of the cab but with type 2A tenders.

CLASS 4, 2-6-0 Tender Engines
Nos. 76000 ~ 76114

Plate 86 No. 76020, the first of the Doncaster batch of Class 4 2-6-0s, with no draught screens or footsteps on the rear of the tender. This class was basically identical to the single chimney **BR**-built version of the Ivatt Class 4 2-6-0, originally introduced as a double-chimney design on the **LMS** in 1947, but modified in its detail parts and fittings to conform with **BR** standard practice. The tender is type **BR 2**, as also fitted to the Class 4 4-6-0s, but without water pick-up apparatus.

British Rail

BRITISH RAILWAYS STANDARD, CLASS 4, 2-6-0 Tender Engine

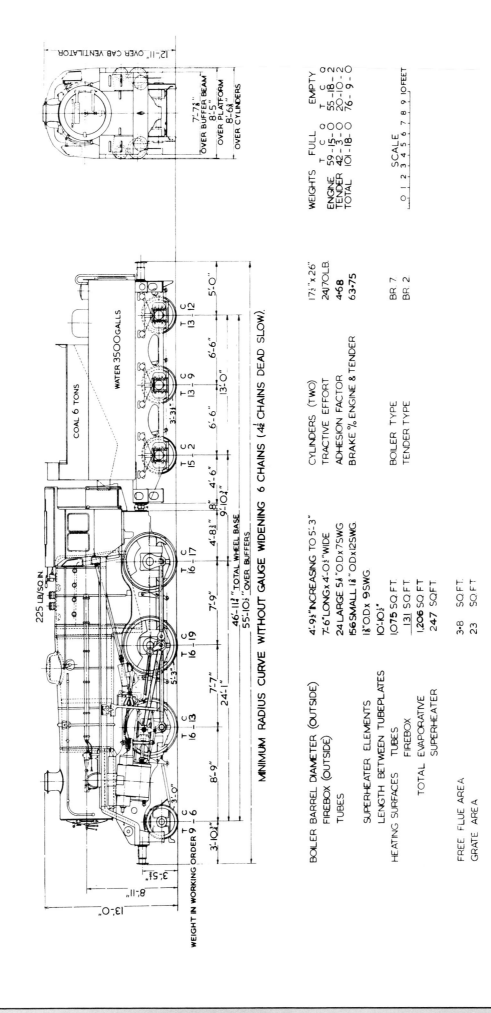

WEIGHTS	FULL	EMPTY
	T C	T C
ENGINE	59-15-0	55-18-2
TENDER	42-3-0	20-10-2
TOTAL	101-18-0	76-9-0

SCALE
0 1 2 3 4 5 6 7 8 9 10FEET

MINIMUM RADIUS CURVE WITHOUT GAUGE WIDENING 6 CHAINS (4½ CHAINS DEAD SLOW).

CYLINDERS (TWO)	17½" x 26"	
TRACTIVE EFFORT	24170LB.	
ADHESION FACTOR	4·68	
BRAKE % ENGINE & TENDER	63·75	
BOILER TYPE	BR 7	
TENDER TYPE	BR 2	

BOILER BARREL DIAMETER (OUTSIDE)	4'-9¾"INCREASING TO 5'-3"	
FIREBOX (OUTSIDE)	7'-6"LONG x 4'-0¾"WIDE	
TUBES	24 LARGE 5⅛"OD x 7SWG	
	156 SMALL 1⅞"OD x 12SWG.	
SUPERHEATER ELEMENTS	1⅜"OD x 9SWG	
LENGTH BETWEEN TUBEPLATES	10'-10½"	
HEATING SURFACES TUBES	1,075 SQ FT.	
FIREBOX	131 SQ FT	
TOTAL EVAPORATIVE	1,206 SQ FT	
SUPERHEATER	247 SQFT	
FREE FLUE AREA	3·8 SQ FT.	
GRATE AREA	23 SQ FT	

WATER 3500 GALLS

COAL 6 TONS

225 LB/SQ.IN

WEIGHT IN WORKING ORDER 9-6

Plate 87 Drawing for Nos. 76000-44.

Plate 88 (below) One of the North Eastern Region allocation, No. 76046, at Penrith on 9th July, 1961, awaiting departure with the 19.20 to Darlington via Kirkby Stephen. It is fitted with AWS apparatus and has rectangular-section (instead of fluted) coupling rods.

Author

Plate 89 The first of the Class 4 2-6-0s, No. 76000, at Horwich Works on completion in 1953, before dispatch to the Scottish Region. *British Rail*

Plate 90 No. 76040 running into Towyn station on 2nd July, 1966 with the 10.30 from Pwllheli to Paddington. *T. J. Edgington*

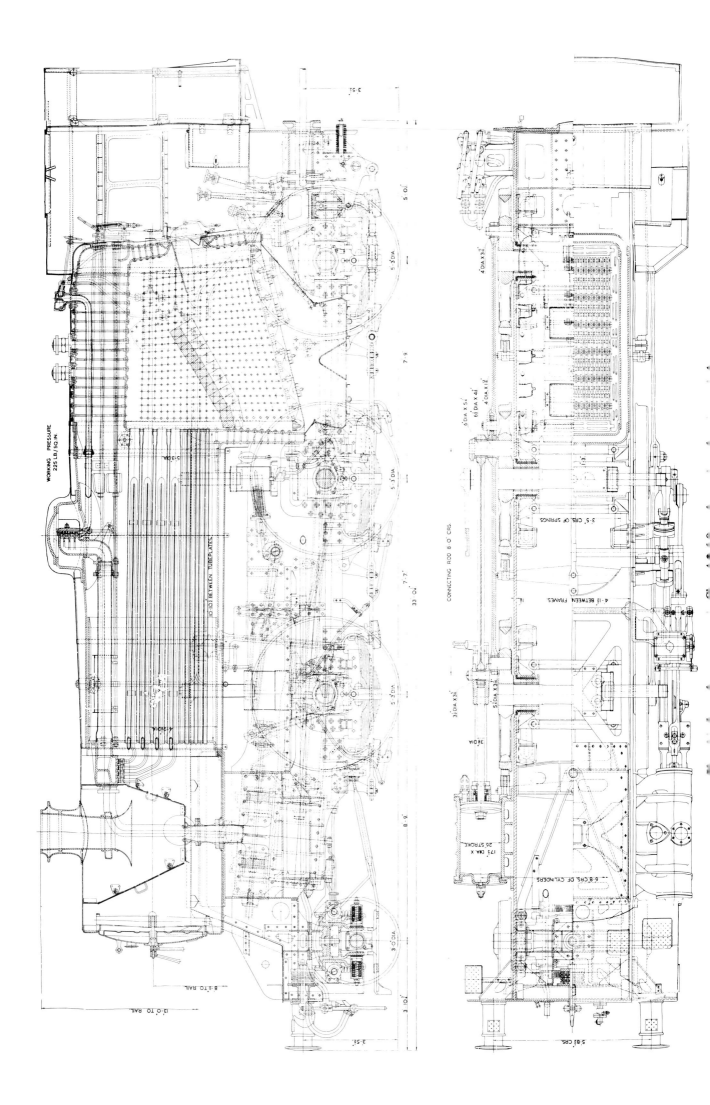

Plate 92 No. 76019, one of the Southern Region allocation, at Eastleigh shed in the late 1950s. The SR engines had additional lamp-irons on the front of the smokebox.

J. H. Russell

Plate 93 No. 76005 at Southampton Central on 20th May, 1966 with a passenger train from Bournemouth.

T. J. Edgington

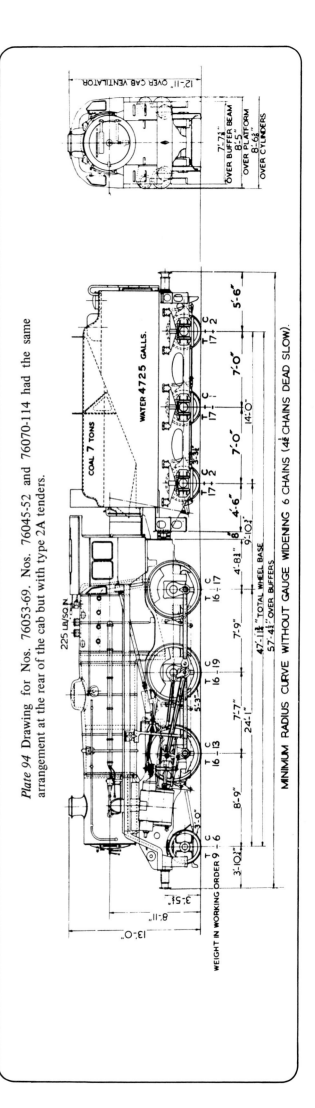

Plate 94 Drawing for Nos. 76053-69. Nos. 76045-52 and 76070-114 had the same arrangement at the rear of the cab but with type 2A tenders.

CLASS 3, 2-6-0 Tender Engines
Nos. 77000 ~ 77019

Plate 95 Except for the ten 'Clans', the Class 3 2-6-0s were the least numerous of the Standard types, all twenty being built at Swindon in 1954. They were the tender counterparts of the Class 3 2-6-2 tank engines. Both classes had the same boiler, type BR 6, which was based on the GWR boiler fitted on the '5100' class 2-6-2 tank engines and other classes. Here, No. 77001 is posed for the official photographer on completion. It incorporates from new various features which were later modifications on other classes: the rectangular-section coupling rods, speedometer and footsteps on the rear of the tender.
British Rail

BRITISH RAILWAYS STANDARD, *CLASS 3, 2-6-0 Tender Engine*

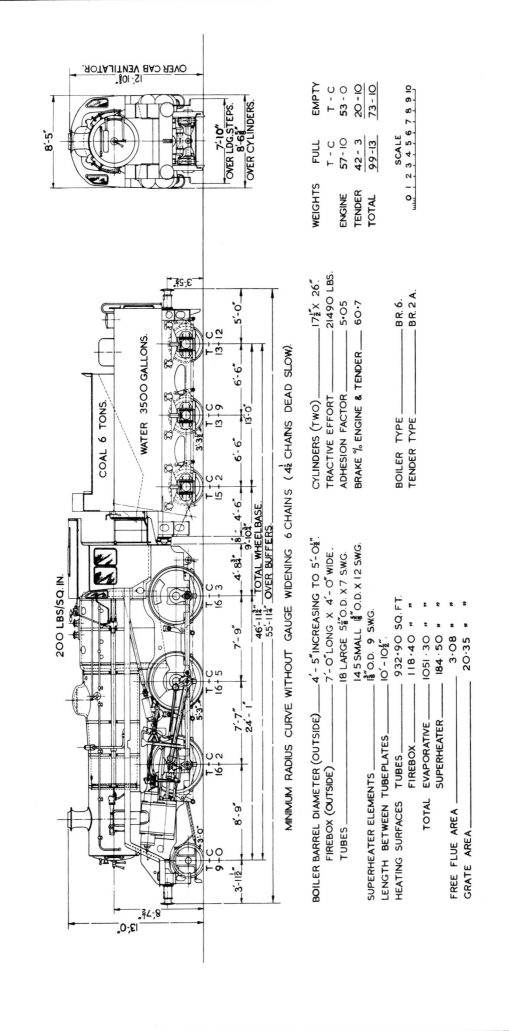

WEIGHTS

	FULL	EMPTY
	T - C	T - C
ENGINE	57 - 10	53 - 0
TENDER	42 - 3	20 - 10
TOTAL	99 - 13	73 - 10

SCALE
0 1 2 3 4 5 6 7 8 9 10

OVER CAB VENTILATOR.
12'-10⅞"

8'-5"

7'-10" OVER LDG. STEPS.
8'-6⅝"
OVER CYLINDERS.

3'-5⅜"

COAL 6 TONS.

WATER 3500 GALLONS.

200 LBS/SQ. IN.

13'-0"
8'-7¾"

T-C 9-0	T-C 16-2	T-C 16-5	T-C 16-3		T-C 15-2	T-C 13-9	T-C 13-12		

3'-11½"   8'-9"   7'-7"   7'-9"   4'-8¼"   8'-   4'-6"   6'-6"   6'-6"   5'-0"
5'-3"   9'-10¾"
24'-1"   13'-0"
46'-11¾" TOTAL WHEELBASE.
55'-11¼" OVER BUFFERS.

MINIMUM RADIUS CURVE WITHOUT GAUGE WIDENING 6 CHAINS (4½ CHAINS DEAD SLOW).

CYLINDERS (TWO)	17½" X 26".
TRACTIVE EFFORT	21490 LBS.
ADHESION FACTOR	5·05
BRAKE % ENGINE & TENDER	60·7
BOILER TYPE	BR. 6.
TENDER TYPE	BR. 2 A.

BOILER BARREL DIAMETER (OUTSIDE)	4'- 5" INCREASING TO 5'- 0½".
FIREBOX (OUTSIDE)	7'- 0" LONG X 4'- 0" WIDE.
TUBES	18 LARGE 5⅛" O.D. X 7 SWG.
	145 SMALL 1½" O.D. X 12 SWG.
SUPERHEATER ELEMENTS	1⅝" O.D. 9 SWG.
LENGTH BETWEEN TUBEPLATES	10'- 10¼".
HEATING SURFACES TUBES	932·90 SQ. FT.
FIREBOX	118·40 "
TOTAL EVAPORATIVE	1051·30 "
SUPERHEATER	184·50 "
FREE FLUE AREA	3·08 "
GRATE AREA	20·35 "

Plate 96

Plate 97 A rear view of No. 77001. The tender is type **BR 2A**. These engines were probably the least known of all the Standard classes. Ten were allocated to the North Eastern Region and ten to the Scottish, and they were generally used on branches well away from the main lines.

British Rail

Plate 99 A view of the right-hand side of No. 77009. This engine had polished rods, tyres and cylinder covers, for exhibition in the roundhouse at Willesden shed during the International Railway Congress in May 1954.

British Rail

Plate 100 On 8th April 1966 No. 77005 has arrived at Kingsmill Colliery with a Stephenson Locomotive Society special. This engine had acquired a Class 4 chimney by this time, which was shorter than was standard. It has been fitted with AWS apparatus and has its depot allocation stencilled on the buffer beam. This latter feature was LNER practice and was perpetuated in Scotland in BR days by Cowlairs Works, which so treated all engines sent for overhaul, irrespective of their origins.

T. J. Edgington

Plate 98 View of the cab of No. 77009. These engines had the re-designed cab and tender arrangement from new. A fall-plate on the front of the tender rested on the cab floor and gangway doors were fitted to the tender and not the cab.

British Rail

Plate 101 No. 77008 at Polmadie shed, Glasgow, on 21st April, 1957.

L. King

Plate 102 No. 77019 at Hurlford shed on 18th September, 1954.

L. King

CLASS 2, 2-6-0 Tender Engines
Nos. 78000 ~ 78064

Plate 103 The Class 2 2-6-0s were basically the same as the LMS 2F 2-6-0s, introduced by H. G. Ivatt in 1946 and perpetuated by BR as Nos. 46400-527, but were modified with BR standard fittings. This view shows No. 78030 of Crewe North shed about 1960, with electrification warning flashes and tender roller-bearing axleboxes painted yellow with horizontal red stripes.

J. B. Bucknall

BRITISH RAILWAYS STANDARD, *CLASS 2, 2-6-0 Tender Engine*

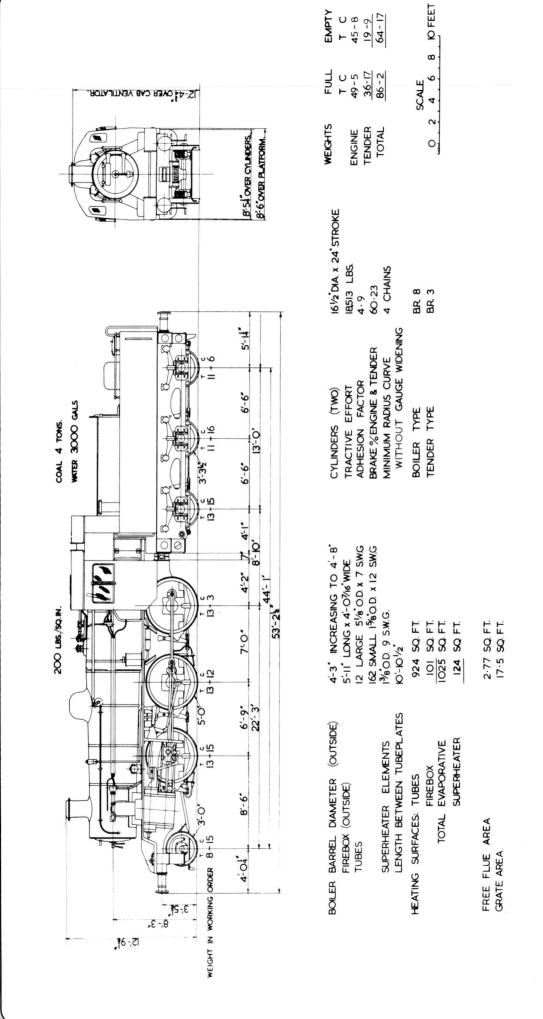

COAL 4 TONS.
WATER 3000 GALS

200 LBS./SQ.IN.

WEIGHTS	FULL		EMPTY	
	T C		T C	
ENGINE	49-5		45-8	
TENDER	36-17		19-9	
TOTAL	86-2		64-17	

SCALE
0 2 4 6 8 IO FEET

CYLINDERS (TWO)	16½" DIA. x 24" STROKE
TRACTIVE EFFORT	18513 LBS.
ADHESION FACTOR	4·9
BRAKE % ENGINE & TENDER	60·23
MINIMUM RADIUS CURVE	4 CHAINS
WITHOUT GAUGE WIDENING	
BOILER TYPE	BR 8
TENDER TYPE	BR 3

BOILER BARREL DIAMETER (OUTSIDE)	4-3" INCREASING TO 4-8"
FIREBOX (OUTSIDE)	5'-11" LONG x 4'-0⁷⁄₁₆"WIDE
TUBES	12 LARGE 5⅛ OD. x 7 SWG
	162 SMALL 1⅝ OD. x 12 SWG
SUPERHEATER ELEMENTS	1⅜ OD. 9 S.W.G.
LENGTH BETWEEN TUBEPLATES	10'-10½"
HEATING SURFACES: TUBES	924 SQ. FT.
FIREBOX	101 SQ. FT.
TOTAL EVAPORATIVE	1025 SQ. FT.
SUPERHEATER	124 SQ. FT.
FREE FLUE AREA	2·77 SQ. FT.
GRATE AREA.	17·5 SQ. FT.

12·4½" OVER CAB VENTILATOR.
8'·5½" OVER CYLINDERS.
8'·6" OVER PLATFORM.

WEIGHT IN WORKING ORDER

4'-0¼"   8'-6"   6'-9"   7'-0"   4'-2"   8'-10"   6'-6"   6'-6"   5'-1¼"
        22'-3"   44'-1"
                    53'-2½"

T C 8-15   T C 13-15   T C 13-12   T C 13-3   T C 13-15   T C 11-16   T C 11-6

3'-0"   5'-0"   4'-1"   3'-3½"   13'-0"

3'-5½"
8'-3"
12'-9½"

Plate 104

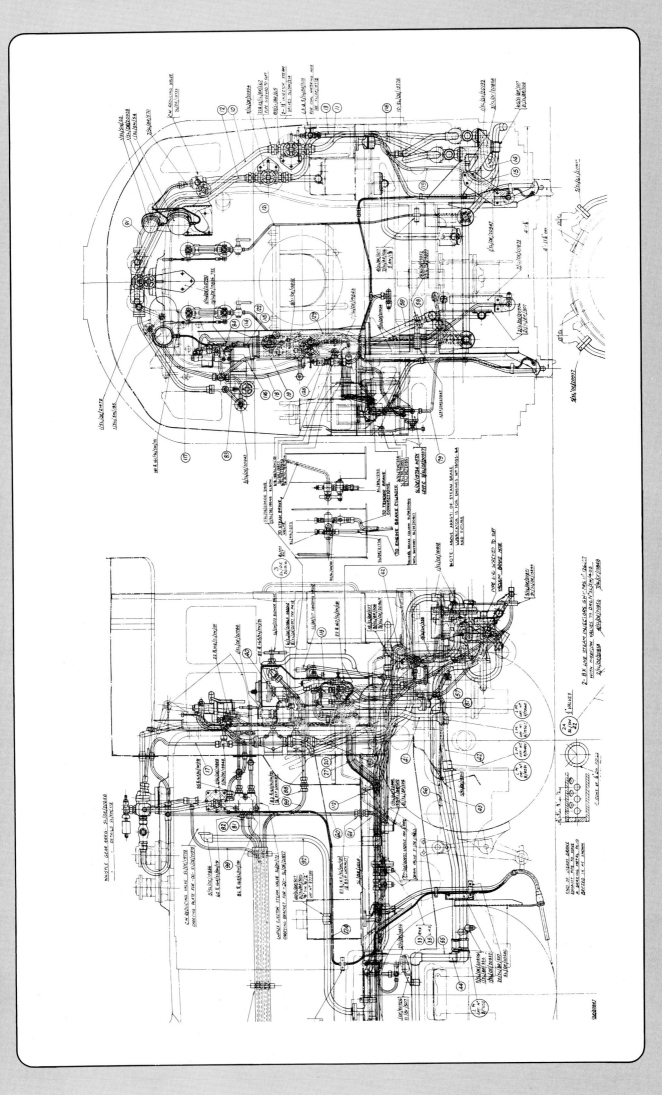

Plate 105 Drawing showing arrangement of injectors, brakes, whistle and other cab fittings.

Plate 106 The first of the Class 2 2-6-0s, No. 78000, built at Darlington early in 1953 for the Western Region.
British Rail

Plate 107 One of the final batch built in 1955, No. 78053 shunting at Gleneagles on 6th June, 1963. It has rectangular-section coupling rods instead of the fluted type of the original batch, electrification warning flashes and a speedometer driven off the rear driving wheel.
Author

CLASS 4, 2-6-4 Tank Engines
Nos. 80000 ~ 80154

Plate 108 The first of the Derby-built Class 4 2-6-4 tank engines, No. 80000, though the first actually built was No. 80010, at Brighton for the Southern Region. These engines were based on the LMS Fairburn Class 4P 2-6-4 tanks but the design had to be modified with higher boiler pressure and smaller cylinders to meet the restrictions of the BR L1 loading gauge.

British Rail

BRITISH RAILWAYS STANDARD, CLASS 4, 2-6-4 Tank Engine

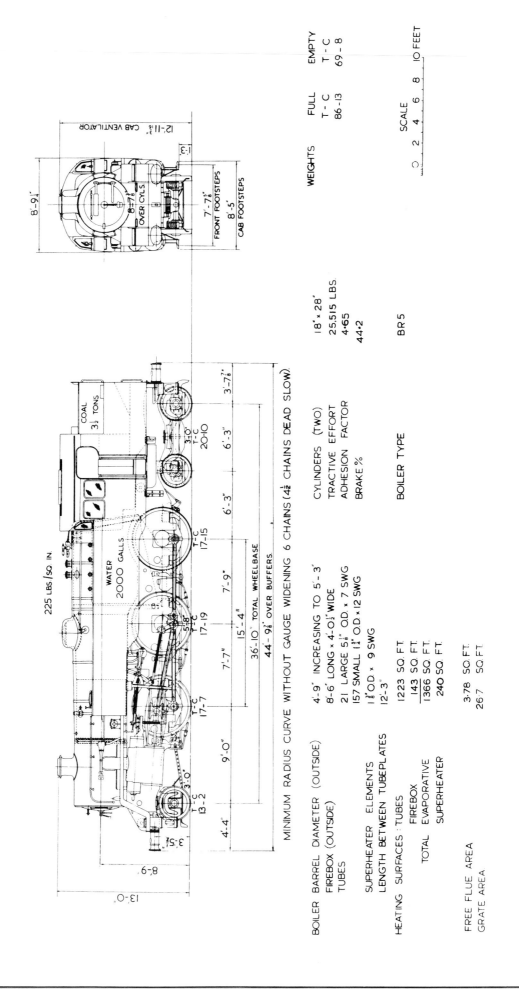

		FULL	EMPTY
		T - C	T - C
WEIGHTS		86-13	69 - 8

CYLINDERS (TWO)	18" × 28"
TRACTIVE EFFORT	25,515 LBS
ADHESION FACTOR	4·65
BRAKE %	44·2
BOILER TYPE	BR 5

SCALE	
0 2 4 6 8 10 FEET	

BOILER BARREL DIAMETER (OUTSIDE)	4'-9" INCREASING TO 5'- 3"
FIREBOX (OUTSIDE)	8'-6" LONG × 4'-0½" WIDE
TUBES	21 LARGE 5⅝" O.D. × 7 SWG
	157 SMALL 1¾" O.D.×12 SWG
SUPERHEATER ELEMENTS	1⅛" O.D × 9 SWG
LENGTH BETWEEN TUBEPLATES	12'-3"
HEATING SURFACES : TUBES	1223 SQ. FT.
FIREBOX	143 SQ. FT.
TOTAL EVAPORATIVE	1366 SQ. FT.
SUPERHEATER	240 SQ. FT.
FREE FLUE AREA	3·78 SQ. FT.
GRATE AREA	26·7 SQ.FT

MINIMUM RADIUS CURVE WITHOUT GAUGE WIDENING 6 CHAINS (4½ CHAINS DEAD SLOW).

225 LBS / SQ IN

COAL 3½ TONS

WATER 2000 GALLS

Plate 109

Plate 110 No. 80067 at Derby after overhaul in the works about 1960.

J.B. Bucknall

Plate 111 No. 80079 at **Bridgnorth** in March 1978. The engine is an excellent example of preservation at its best — beautifully restored to **BR** condition and superbly kept, but without any unauthentic features.
Author

Plates 112 and 113 Two views of the rear of No. 80079 at Bridgnorth in March 1978.
Author

Plate 114 The last of the class to be built, No. 80154, at Newhaven shed on 13th April, 1958. The return crank is mounted on four studs, LMS-style, instead of on a square pin.

L. King

Plates 115 and 116 Two views inside the cab of No. 80079, as preserved on the Severn Valley Railway in March 1978. Unlike both the 'mangle-wheel' reverser of the early Standard tender engines and the conventional arrangement with the reversing wheel at right angles to the shaft, the wheel on these engines was at 45° to the shaft.

Author

Plate 117 Another view of No. 80154 taken on the same day at Brighton shed.   *L. King*

Plate 118 A view looking down on No. 80079 at **Bridgnorth** on 27th March, 1978, showing the detail on the top of the engine.

Author

CLASS 3, 2-6-2 Tank Engines
Nos. 82000 ~ 82044

Plate 119 The first of the Class 3 tank engines, No. 82000, on completion at Swindon in 1951 for service on the Western Region. It is finished in the Standard lined black and has fluted coupling rods.   *British Rail*

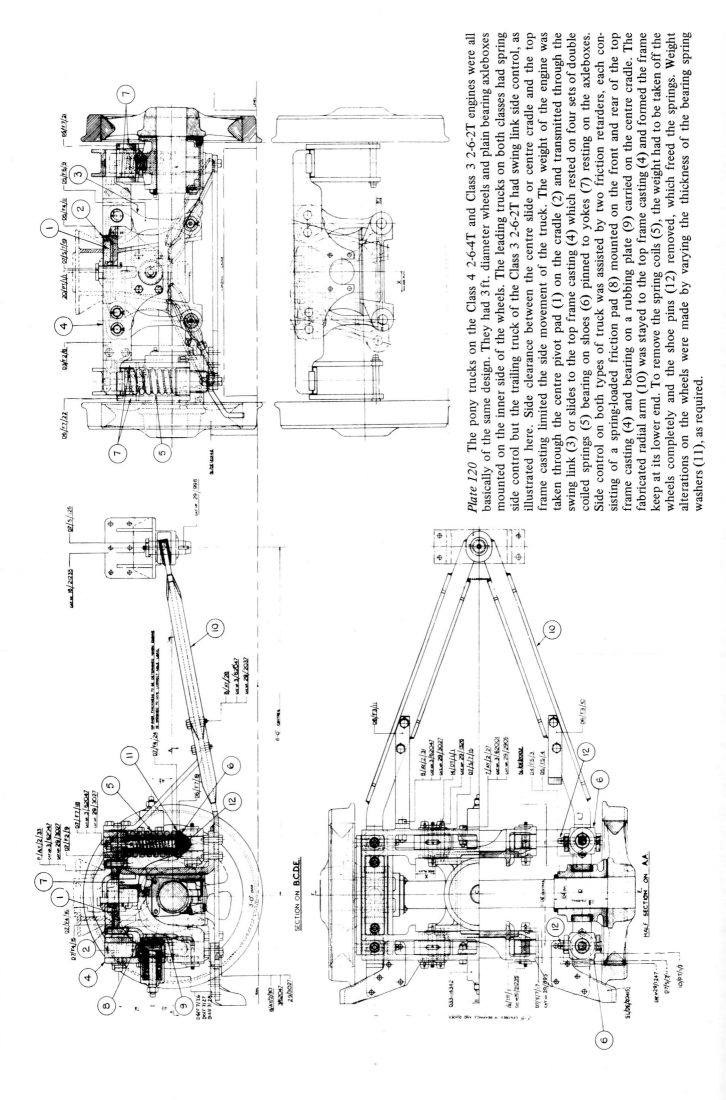

Plate 120 The pony trucks on the Class 4 2-6-4T and Class 3 2-6-2T engines were all basically of the same design. They had 3ft. diameter wheels and plain bearing axleboxes mounted on the inner side of the wheels. The leading trucks on both classes had spring side control but the trailing truck of the Class 3 2-6-2T had swing link side control, as illustrated here. Side clearance between the centre slide or centre cradle and the top frame casting limited the side movement of the truck. The weight of the engine was taken through the centre pivot pad (1) on the cradle (2) and transmitted through the swing link (3) or slides to the top frame casting (4) which rested on four sets of double coiled springs (5) bearing on shoes (6) pinned to yokes (7) resting on the axleboxes. Side control on both types of truck was assisted by two friction retarders, each consisting of a spring-loaded friction pad (8) mounted on the front and rear of the top frame casting (4) and bearing on a rubbing plate (9) carried on the centre cradle. The fabricated radial arm (10) was stayed to the top frame casting (4) and formed the frame keep at its lower end. To remove the spring coils (5), the weight had to be taken off the wheels completely and the shoe pins (12) removed, which freed the springs. Weight alterations on the wheels were made by varying the thickness of the bearing spring washers (11), as required.

BRITISH RAILWAYS STANDARD, *CLASS 3, 2-6-2 Tank Engine*

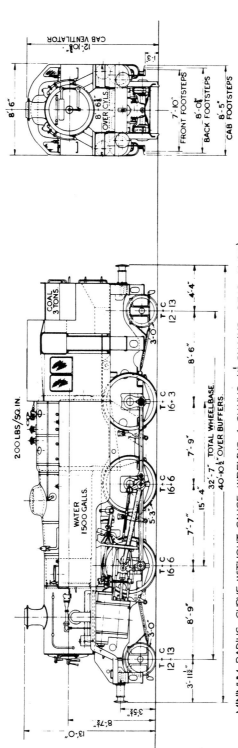

MINIMUM RADIUS CURVE WITHOUT GAUGE WIDENING 6 CHAINS (4½ CHAINS DEAD SLOW).

BOILER BARREL DIAMETER (OUTSIDE)	4'-5" INCREASING TO 5'-0½".
FIREBOX (OUTSIDE)	7'-0" LONG X 4'-0" WIDE.
TUBES	18 LARGE 5⅝" O.D. x 7 S.W.G.
	145 SMALL 1⅝" O.D. x 12 S.W.G.
SUPERHEATER ELEMENTS	⅞" O.D. 9 S.W.G.
LENGTH BETWEEN TUBEPLATES	10-10½".
HEATING SURFACES. TUBES	932·90 SQ.FT
FIREBOX	118·40 " "
TOTAL EVAPORATIVE	1051·30 " "
SUPERHEATER	184·50 " "
FREE FLUE AREA	3·08 " "
GRATE AREA	20·35 " "

CYLINDERS (TWO)	17½" x 26".
TRACTIVE EFFORT	21490 LBS.
ADHESION FACTOR	5·08
BRAKE % ENGINE	51·5
BOILER TYPE	BR 6.

WEIGHTS.	FULL.	EMPTY.
	T - C	T - C
	74 - 1.	60 - 18.

SCALE

0 2 4 6 8 10 FEET

Plate 121

Plate 123 Rear view of No. 82000, showing inset coal bunker for good vision when running bunker-first, and Western Region lamp-irons. *British Rail*

Plate 122 A left-side view of No. 82000 when new. These engines were the tank-engine counterparts of the Class 3 2-6-0s, Nos. 77000-19. *British Rail*

Plate 124 No. 82037 in the Swindon green livery introduced in 1956, with black and orange lining and a single orange line along the lower edge of the side of the running plate. It has rectangular-section coupling rods and a speedometer.

British Rail

Plate 125 No. 82042 passing Pensford & Bromley Collieries Sidings signal box with the 16.50 Sundays only from Bristol to Frome on 13th September, 1959, the last day of Sunday working.

Hugh Ballantyne

Plate 126 The last of the class, No. 82044, at Shrewsbury on 20th April, 1963. It has the usual modifications such as rectangular-section coupling rods and speedometer but has not been given the WR green livery. In fact, it has a modified version of the lined black mixed-traffic livery, with the number on the cab side, instead of the bunker, and no lining on the bunker, as standard on the Class 2 2-6-2 tanks.

Author

Plate 127 No. 82024 at Nine Elms on 25th May, 1963, with rectangular-section coupling rods. Southern Region lamp-irons and small lifting brackets on the cab roof. The yellow triangle below the number signifies that the engine has the French TIA water-treatment system adopted by the Southern. On the right is a Standard Class 5 4-6-0 with an ordinary whistle in place of the usual chime whistle behind the chimney.   *Author*

CLASS 2, 2-6-2 Tank Engines
Nos. 84000 ~ 84029

Plate 128 The Standard Class 2 2-6-2 tank engines were based on the LMS Class 2P 2-6-2Ts, introduced by H.G. Ivatt in 1946 and perpetuated by BR, eventually becoming Nos. 41200-329, but the design was modified in its details to incorporate BR standard fittings. Here, No. 84002 is seen on completion at Crewe Works. It is in the lined black mixed-traffic livery, has fluted coupling rods and speedometer, and is fitted with push-and-pull apparatus (beside the smokebox).

British Rail

BRITISH RAILWAYS STANDARD, CLASS 2, 2-6-2 Tank Engine

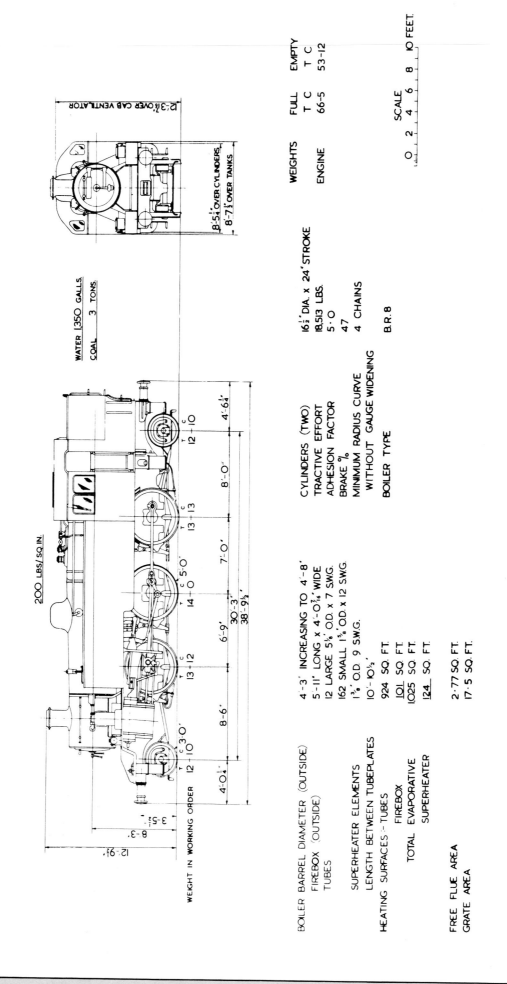

200 LBS/SQ IN.

12'-3⅜" OVER CAB VENTILATOR

8'-5¼" OVER CYLINDERS
8'-7½" OVER TANKS

WATER 1350 GALLS.
COAL   3 TONS.

WEIGHT IN WORKING ORDER

4'-0¼" 8'-6" 6'-9" 7'-0" 8'-0" 4'-6¼"
30'-3"
38'-9½"

12-10⅟₄ 13-12 14-0 13-13 12-10
 T C   T C   5-0   T C   T C

3'-5½"
8'-3"
12'-9½"

BOILER BARREL DIAMETER (OUTSIDE)	4'-3" INCREASING TO 4'-8"
FIREBOX (OUTSIDE)	5'-11" LONG x 4'-0⅞" WIDE
TUBES	12 LARGE 5⅛" O.D. x 7 SWG.
	162 SMALL 1⅜" O.D. x 12 SWG.
SUPERHEATER ELEMENTS	1⅜" O.D. 9 SWG.
LENGTH BETWEEN TUBEPLATES	10'-10½"
HEATING SURFACES :- TUBES	924 SQ. FT.
FIREBOX	101 SQ. FT.
TOTAL EVAPORATIVE	1025 SQ. FT.
SUPERHEATER	124 SQ. FT.
FREE FLUE AREA	2·77 SQ. FT.
GRATE AREA	17·5 SQ. FT.

CYLINDERS (TWO)	16½" DIA. x 24" STROKE
TRACTIVE EFFORT	18,513 LBS.
ADHESION FACTOR	5·0
BRAKE %	47
MINIMUM RADIUS CURVE	4 CHAINS
WITHOUT GAUGE WIDENING	
BOILER TYPE	B.R.8

WEIGHTS	FULL	EMPTY
	T C	T C
ENGINE	66-5	53-12

SCALE
O 2 4 6 8 IO FEET.

Plate 129

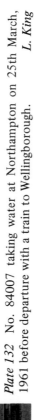

Plate 130 A broadside view of No. 84002. The footsteps at the rear of the bunker and the two hand-rails above them were not a feature of the LMS 2-6-2T design.

British Rail

Plate 131 (bottom left) No. 84021 at Hither Green on 11th May, 1957. The return crank is mounted on four studs instead of a square pin, as in the first batch, and it has the larger cab-side numbers of a Darlington-built engine.

L. King

Plate 132 No. 84007 taking water at Northampton on 25th March, 1961 before departure with a train to Wellingborough.

L. King

Plate 133 On 31st March, 1957, No. 84001 stands
at Chester Northgate shed.
L. King

Plate 134 A view of No. 84015, in something less than immaculate condition. It has the pre-1956 emblem and the tank has suffered a dent from a slight collision.

J. B. Bucknall

Plate 135 No. 84029 at New Romsey with a train to Ashford on 16th August, 1959. It has the larger numbers of a Darlington-built engine.

L. King

CLASS 9F, 2-10-0 Tender Engines
Nos. 92000 ~ 92250

Plate 136 The first of the Class 9F 2-10-0s, No. 92000, on completion at Crewe Works in January 1954. It has Western Region lamp-irons for allocation to Ebbw Junction. The '9Fs' had from new many of the features applied to other Standard engines as later modifications, such as rectangular-section coupling rods and footsteps on the top of the rear of the tender. None were ever fitted with speedometers. The tender is type BR 1G holding 7 tons of coal and 5,000 gallons of water.

British Rail

BRITISH RAILWAYS STANDARD, *CLASS 9, 2-10-0 Tender Engine*

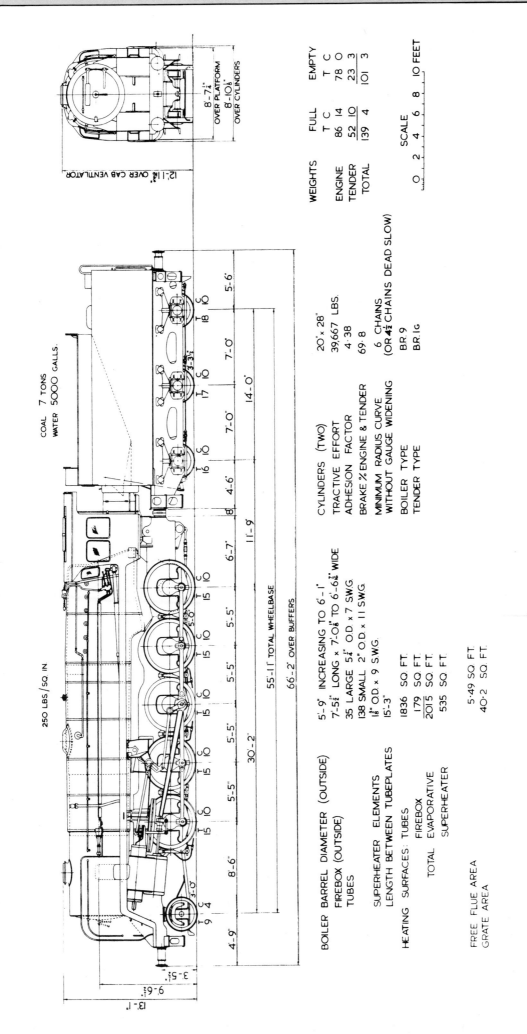

WEIGHTS	FULL		EMPTY	
	T	C	T	C
ENGINE	86	14	78	0
TENDER	52	10	23	3
TOTAL	139	4	101	3

SCALE

0 2 4 6 8 10 FEET

CYLINDERS (TWO)	20" x 28"
TRACTIVE EFFORT	39,667 LBS.
ADHESION FACTOR	4·38
BRAKE % ENGINE & TENDER	69·8
MINIMUM RADIUS CURVE WITHOUT GAUGE WIDENING	6 CHAINS (OR 4½ CHAINS DEAD SLOW)
BOILER TYPE	BR 9
TENDER TYPE	BR.1G

250 LBS/SQ IN

COAL 7 TONS
WATER 5000 GALLS.

BOILER BARREL DIAMETER (OUTSIDE)	5'-9" INCREASING TO 6'-1"
FIREBOX (OUTSIDE)	7'-5½" LONG x 7'-0⅜" TO 6'-6¼" WIDE
TUBES	35 LARGE 5¼" OD x 7 SWG.
	138 SMALL 2" OD x 11 SWG
SUPERHEATER ELEMENTS	1⅜" OD x 9 SWG.
LENGTH BETWEEN TUBEPLATES	15'-3"
HEATING SURFACES: TUBES	1836 SQ FT.
FIREBOX	179 SQ FT.
TOTAL EVAPORATIVE	2015 SQ FT.
SUPERHEATER	535 SQ FT.
FREE FLUE AREA	5·49 SQ FT.
GRATE AREA	40·2 SQ. FT.

Plate 137 Drawing for the first batch of Class 9F 2-10-0s, Nos. 92000-9. All subsequent batches with single chimneys differed only in the type of tender fitted and in minor details.

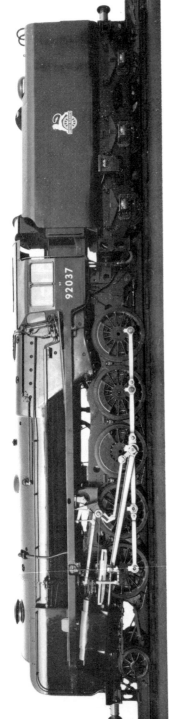

Plate 138 No. 92037 as built, with BR 1F tender holding 7 tons of coal and 5,625 gallons of water.
British Rail

Plate 139 (bottom left) Head-on view of No. 92083 of 15A shed (Wellingborough) at Willesden Junction shed on 10th March, 1963. It has acquired a single wide footstep under the smokebox and is in fairly typical condition for a workaday 9F. *Author*

Plate 140 (below) Another Midland Class 9F, No. 92115, at Kettering shed on 19th April, 1963, with **BR** 1C tender holding 9 tons of coal and 4,725 gallons of water. The flangeless centre driving wheels can be clearly seen. The 9Fs took over the hardest duties on the Midland main line from the ex-LMS Garratts and Stanier Class 8F 2-8-0s. *Author*

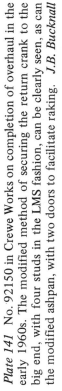

Plate 141 No. 92150 in Crewe Works on completion of overhaul in the early 1960s. The modified method of securing the return crank to the big end, with four studs in the LMS fashion, can be clearly seen, as can the modified ashpan, with two doors to facilitate raking. *J.B. Bucknall*

Plate 142 On 21st September, 1965, No. 92062 takes water at Consett before returning to South Pelaw for the second half of the train of iron ore which it had worked from Tyne Dock. Ten Class 9Fs, Nos. 92060-6 and 92097-9, were fitted with the necessary equipment to work the special wagons provided for the Tyne Dock–Consett iron-ore traffic. Each engine had two 10 in. Westinghouse air compressors, mounted on the right-hand side, which maintained a pressure of 90 psi when the wagons were loaded and also operated the wagon doors.

Hugh Ballantyne

Plate 143 Ten Class 9Fs, Nos. 92020-9, were built in 1955 with Franco-Crosti boilers, an Italian design intended to achieve higher efficiency. This view shows the right-hand side of No. 92024, with BR 1B tender (7 tons of coal and 4,725 gallons of water). The chimney in the usual position on the smokebox was used for lighting up only.

British Rail

BRITISH RAILWAYS STANDARD, *CLASS 9, 2-10-0 Crosti Tender Engine*

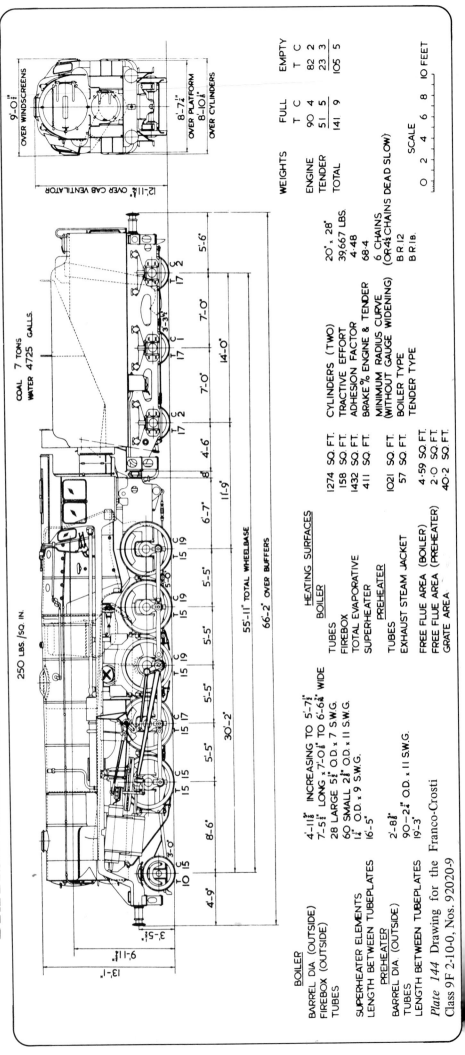

250 LBS./SQ. IN.

COAL 7 TONS
WATER 4725 GALLS.

WEIGHTS	FULL		EMPTY	
	T	C	T	C
ENGINE	90	4	82	2
TENDER	51	5	23	3
TOTAL	141	9	105	5

CYLINDERS (TWO)	20″ x 28″
TRACTIVE EFFORT	39,667 LBS.
ADHESION FACTOR	4·48
BRAKE % ENGINE & TENDER	68·4
MINIMUM RADIUS CURVE (WITHOUT GAUGE WIDENING)	6 CHAINS (OR 4½ CHAINS DEAD SLOW)
BOILER TYPE	BR 12
TENDER TYPE	BR 1B.

SCALE

O 2 4 6 8 IO FEET

HEATING SURFACES

BOILER

TUBES	1274	SQ. FT.
FIREBOX	158	SQ. FT.
TOTAL EVAPORATIVE	1432	SQ. FT.
SUPERHEATER	411	SQ. FT.

PREHEATER

TUBES	1021	SQ. FT.
EXHAUST STEAM JACKET	57	SQ. FT.
FREE FLUE AREA (BOILER)	4·59	SQ. FT.
FREE FLUE AREA (PREHEATER)	2·0	SQ. FT.
GRATE AREA	40·2	SQ. FT.

BOILER

BARREL DIA (OUTSIDE)	4′-11¼″ INCREASING TO 5′-7½″
FIREBOX (OUTSIDE)	7′-5½″ LONG x 7′-0⅛″ TO 6′-6¾″ WIDE
TUBES	28 LARGE 5⅛″ O.D. x 7 S.W.G.
	60 SMALL 2⅛″ O.D. x 11 S.W.G.
SUPERHEATER ELEMENTS	1¼″ O.D. x 9 S.W.G.
LENGTH BETWEEN TUBEPLATES	16′-5″

PREHEATER

BARREL DIA (OUTSIDE)	2′-8⅞″
TUBES	90–2¼″ O.D. x 11 S.W.G.
LENGTH BETWEEN TUBEPLATES	19′-3″

Plate 144 Drawing for the Franco-Crosti Class 9F 2-10-0, Nos. 92020-9

Plate 145 The Franco-Crosti boiler was intended to achieve higher efficiency by making more use of the heat both of combustion and of the exhaust steam. Basically, the hot gases from the firebox passed through the main boiler in the usual way but were then directed downwards to pass back through a pre-heater before exhausting on the right-hand side of the engine. This view shows one of the boilers in Crewe Works, with the main boiler above and the pre-heater drum below.

British Rail

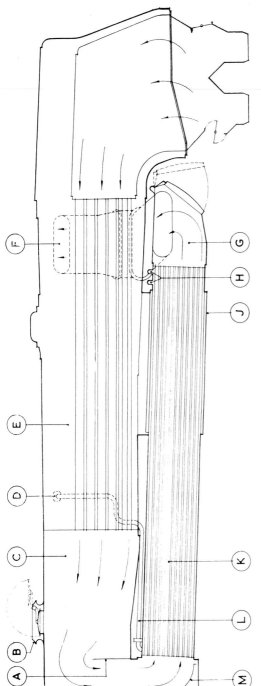

Plate 146 Diagram of Crosti boiler principle as applied to **B.R.** 2-10-0 locomotives.

A. Upper deflector
B. Lighting-up chimney
C. Front smokebox
D. Top feed
E. Main boiler
F. Final chimney (r.h.s.)
G. Final smokebox
H. Feed to preheater
J. Exhaust steam jacket
K. Preheater
L. Water: preheater to main boiler
M. Lower deflector

Note:– Path of combustion air and hot gases indicated thus

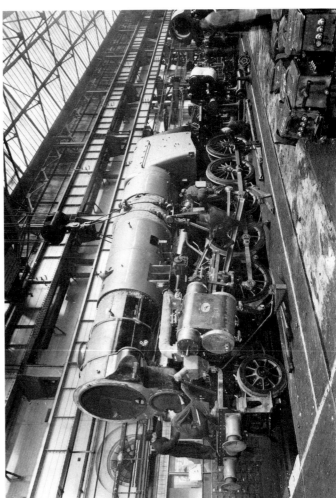

Plates 147 and 148 These two views show further constructional stages of the Franco-*British Rail* Crosti boilered 2-10-0s.

Plate 150 The front end of No. 92024, showing the two access doors and the pre-heater fitting between the frames. Beside the upper footsteps are the covers of the filler pipes for the leading sandboxes.

British Rail

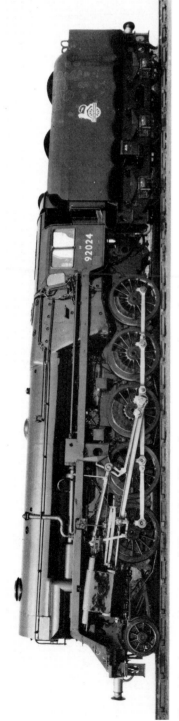

Plate 149 A nearside view of No. 92024. The exhaust-steam pipe from the left-hand cylinder can be clearly seen, as can the tubular drive shaft from the reverser, running horizontally above the running plate. This deviation from standard was necessitated by the positioning of the pre-heater in the space beneath the main boiler and between the frames.

British Rail

Plate 151 A close-up of the offside of No. 92024, showing the chimney of the Franco-Crosti boiler and the main pipe leading exhaust steam to it from the right-hand cylinder. Exhaust steam from the left-hand cylinder passed back in a similar pipe on the other side of the engine, some of it to a steam jacket round the rear of the pre-heater and the rest to cross beneath the boiler to the chimney. When fresh water was fed into the pre-heater, it displaced a similar volume of heated water which passed into the main boiler through the lagged pipe and clack valve seen on the right in this picture. The other pipe and clack valve was for emergency use only, when it conveyed water direct from the live steam injector.

British Rail

Plate 152 After complaints from drivers about visibility being obscured by exhaust steam blowing down in front of the cab, smoke deflectors were fitted to the Franco-Crosti Class 9Fs but were only partially effective. Here, No. 92029 is seen so fitted at Wellingborough shed in January 1956.

K.C.H. Fairey

Plate 153 A view of No. 92028 at work passing Bedford on a down freight in September 1958.

K. C. H. Fairey

Plate 154 Converted Franco-Crosti Class 9F No. 92026 at Stafford shed while running in after a visit to Crewe Works. Both clack valves are on the right side of the boiler, and the irregular shape of both the running plate and the smokebox are other signs of its original condition. The converted engines were never fitted with smoke deflectors.

J. B. Bucknall

Plate 155 A close-up of the driving wheels of a converted Franco-Crosti Class 9F, showing the flangeless centre driving wheel and the original method of securing the return crank to the big end, Gresley style, which was later replaced by the LMS method using four studs.

J.B. Bucknall

BRITISH RAILWAYS STANDARD, CLASS 9, 2-10-0 Tender Engine

FITTED WITH MECHANICAL STOKER

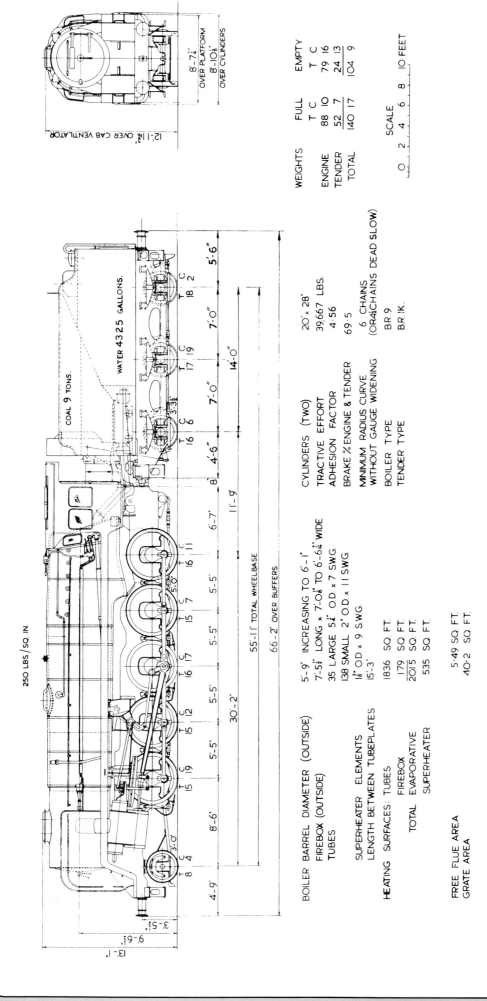

250 LBS / SQ. IN

COAL 9 TONS.

WATER 4325 GALLONS.

8'-7¼" OVER PLATFORM
8'-10⅛" OVER CYLINDERS

12'-11¼" OVER CAB VENTILATOR

WEIGHTS	FULL		EMPTY	
	T	C	T	C
ENGINE	88	10	79	16
TENDER	52	7	24	13
TOTAL	140	17	104	9

SCALE

0 2 4 6 8 10 FEET

BOILER BARREL DIAMETER (OUTSIDE)	5'-9" INCREASING TO 6'-1"
FIREBOX (OUTSIDE)	7'-5⅞" LONG x 7'-0⅞" TO 6'-6⅞" WIDE
TUBES	35 LARGE 5¼" O.D. x 7 SWG
	138 SMALL 2" O.D. x 11 SWG
SUPERHEATER ELEMENTS	1⅜" O.D x 9 SWG.
LENGTH BETWEEN TUBEPLATES	15'-3"
HEATING SURFACES: TUBES	1836 SQ. FT.
FIREBOX	179 SQ. FT.
TOTAL EVAPORATIVE	2015 SQ. FT.
SUPERHEATER	535 SQ. FT.
FREE FLUE AREA	5·49 SQ. FT.
GRATE AREA	40·2 SQ. FT.

CYLINDERS (TWO)	20" x 28"
TRACTIVE EFFORT	39,667 LBS.
ADHESION FACTOR	4·56
BRAKE % ENGINE & TENDER	69·5
MINIMUM RADIUS CURVE WITHOUT GAUGE WIDENING	6 CHAINS (OR 4½ CHAINS DEAD SLOW)
BOILER TYPE	BR. 9
TENDER TYPE	BR. 1K.

Plate 156 A drawing for Class 9F 2-10-0s fitted with mechanical stoker and double chimney. Nos. 92165-7. Except for the stoker and variations in tender type, this drawing applies to all double-chimney 9Fs.

Plate 157 In 1958 three Class 9Fs, Nos. 92165-7, were built new with mechanical stokers and double chimneys to establish how much these features would enhance their haulage capacity. This view shows No. 92167 on completion at Crewe Works. The tender is type BR 1K.
British Rail

Plate 159 View of the cab of a Class 9F 2-10-0 equipped with Berkeley mechanical stoker. The controls for the steam jets distributing the coal in the firebox are grouped on the right under the word 'JETS'.
British Rail

Plate 158 (below) The front of the tender of a stoker-fired Class 9F, showing the intermediate screw and the stoker engine to its left. The fall-plate is in three parts to fit over the screw, but the gangway doors are fitted to the tender in the usual way for the modified Standard tenders.
British Rail

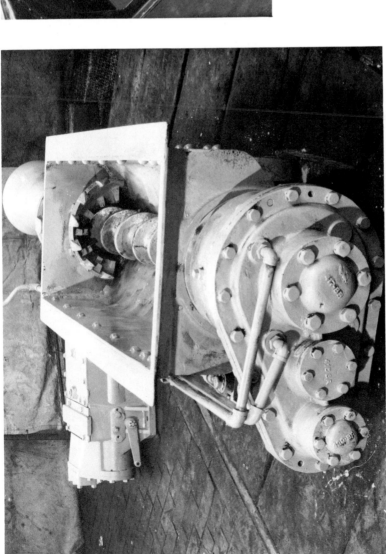

Plate 160 (above) A view through the tender doors to the footplate of a stoker-fired Class 9F, showing the trough and some of the teeth of the crusher. *British Rail*

Plate 161 (upper left) The trough, screw and crusher from the gearbox end, with the stoker engine on the left. The screw and crusher can be seen in the trough. *British Rail*

Plate 162 (lower left) The stoker engine, tubular drive shaft to gearbox, trough and intermediate screw of a Berkeley mechanical stoker before fitting to a BR Class 9F 2-10-0. *British Rail*

Plate 163 No. 92178 on road trials between Reading and Stoke Gifford early in 1958. These trials with an engine experimentally fitted with a double chimney were successful and led to the fitting of this feature to all new 9Fs from No. 92183 onwards. *British Rail*

Plate 164 No. 92000 after the fitting of a double chimney in 1960. By comparison with the view of the engine in original condition, there are only a few minor changes. Although double chimneys were standard on all new 9Fs from No. 92183, less than half a dozen of the single-chimney engines were converted.

British Rail

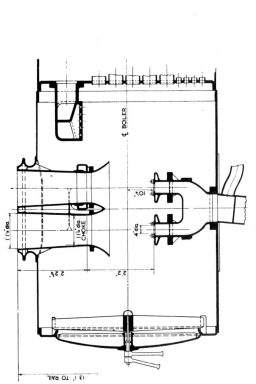

Plate 166 In 1959 No. 92250 was experimentally fitted with a Giesl ejector. There were two aims in view: firstly to try to achieve lower coal consumption with normal grades of coal, and secondly, to see if lower and cheaper grades of coal could be burnt. Some saving of coal was made by comparison with the standard double-chimney 9F, which in turn used 5% less than the single-chimney version, but not enough to persuade **BR** to fit other engines with it. Lower grade coal could not be used reliably. This official view shows No. 92250 shortly after the Giesl ejector was fitted.

British Rail

Plate 167 No. 92250 at Birmingham Snow Hill with a down oil train on 25th April, 1964. It has acquired a single wide footstep under the smokebox. Although the Giesl ejector was not adopted by **BR**, No. 92250 continued to be so fitted until withdrawn.

T. J. Edgington

Plate 165 A smokebox arrangement of a 9F 2-10-0 fitted with double blast-pipe and chimney *(top)* and with Giesl ejector *(bottom)*.

THE EJECTOR CROSS SECTIONAL AREA IS ADJUSTABLE.
FOR BIDWORTH COAL THIS AREA WAS 30·2 SQ. IN.
FOR (WHITWICK LARGE) THIS AREA WAS 26·2 SQ. IN.
(WHITWICK SLACK)
(COSSALL)

GIESL OBLONG EJECTOR DRAUGHT ARRANGEMENT.

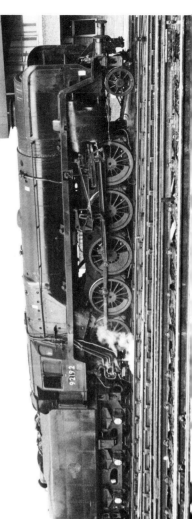

Plate 169 The last steam engine built at Crewe was Class 9F 2-10-0 No. 92250. It is seen here on completion in December 1958, with a double chimney and the return crank secured to the big end by the LMS method using four studs, a modification first introduced on No. 92050 in 1955. A single wide footstep beneath the smokebox was a later modification, replacing the two small steps seen here.

British Rail

Plate 170 No. 92192 at Wolverhampton High Level in the early 1960s. It has electrification warning flashes and the tender is equipped with Timken roller bearings.

J.B. Bucknall

Plate 168 The only 9F to have any livery other than plain unlined black was No. 92220 *Evening Star*, which was the last steam engine built for British Railways and the last steam engine built at Swindon. This was given the lined green livery complete with Great Western copper cap to the chimney. The nameplate was cast, like those of the 'Britannias' and 'Clans' but the lettering was in the same style as GWR nameplates. A competition was held by the Western Region staff magazine to select the name and *Evening Star* was suggested by three entrants.

British Rail

Appendix One

Tenders

The original BR Standard tenders were designated types 1, 2 and 3. Types 1 and 2 were designed to suit the original BR Standard cab layout. This was arranged to make things easier for the crew, particularly the fireman, by having the whole of the cab floor attached to the engine and doing away with the traditional fall-plate between engine and tender. The cab floor was extended further to the rear than on conventional British engines, to come beneath the tender shovelling plate, and there was no fall-plate of any kind. Gangway doors were fitted to the cab between the rear of the cab side-sheets and a rear hand-rail extended from the end of the cab floor to the corner of the roof. Tank capacity was controlled by slots in the water pick-up delivery pipe at the water level, allowing water to flow out of the tender when filled to nominal capacity. Thus the enlarged version of type 1, which held 5,000 instead of 4,250 gallons and was designated type 1A, was, in fact, exactly the same size but with these slots positioned higher. Over-flow indicator pipes were fitted; one at each back corner of the bottom plate of the tender, and a consequence of the whole arrangement was that, unlike traditional British tenders, no overflow occurred through the filling hole. Type 3 was the tender for the Class 2 2-6-0s. As these engines were basically the same as the LMS Ivatt 2F 2-6-0s, they did not have the BR Standard cab layout and so their tenders were virtually the same as their LMS predecessors, having the conventional arrangement with fall-plates.

The original design of BR cab proved to be excessively draughty in service. Air rushing up the front of the tender and round the sides of the rear of the engine had unrestricted access to the interior of the cab itself. Attempts were made to overcome the problem by fitting flexible screens between the rear of the cab and the front of the tender but were only partly effective. Eventually the cab layout was redesigned to produce a proper solution. The one-piece cab floor was retained but a short full-width fall-plate was fitted to the front of the tender so as to rest on the rear of the cab floor. Gangway doors with anti-draught flaps beneath them were fitted to the tenders and there were no hand-rails between the rear of the cab floor and the roof, as shorter grab-rails on the tenders served the same purpose.

All subsequent tenders had this arrangement. Types 1H and 1G were simply the modified versions of types 1 and 1A (4,250 and 5,000 gallons respectively) and type 2A

was the modified version of type 2 but types 1B-1F, 1J and 1K differed in another respect also. On these types the coal bunkers were built out to the full width of the loading gauge, instead of being inset and having front spectacle plates, and the flush sides curved inwards at the top in the manner of the Stanier tenders on the LMS. Despite the apparent multiplicity of types there was little real difference between many of them. Types 1B-1E all held 4,725 gallons of water with a coal capacity of 7, 9 and 10 tons; 1D was merely the coal-pusher version of 1C, and 1E the 10-ton variant of 1D, while 1K was the mechanical-stoker version of the same basic type. Type 1F had the greatest water capacity of all BR tenders, 5,625 gallons, and 1J was the large tender built in 1957 to replace the 1E tender on No. 71000.

The following list shows the engines to which each tender type was fitted:

BR Type	Engine Nos.
1	70000-24, 70030-44, 72000-9, 73000-49
1A	70025-9
1B	73080-9, 73100-9, 73120-34, 73145-71, 75065-79, 76053-69, 92020-9, 92060-6, 92097-9
1C	73065-79, 73090-9, 73135-44, 92015-9, 92045-59, 92077-86, 92100-39, 92150-64
1D	70045-54
1E	71000
1F	73110-9, 92010-4, 92030-44, 92067-76, 92087-96, 92140-9, 92168-202
1G	73050-2, 92000-9, 92203-50
1H	73053-64
1J	71000
1K	92165-7
2	75000-49, 76000-44
2A	75050-64, 76045-52, 76070-114, 77000-19
3	78000-64

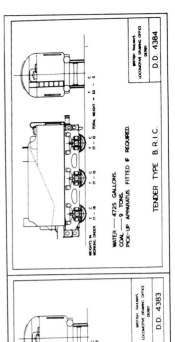

WEIGHTS IN WORKING ORDER 16-9 T C 14-3 T C 16-3 TOTAL WEIGHT 49-3

WATER —— 4250 GALLONS.
COAL —— 7 TONS.
PICK-UP APPARATUS.

TENDER TYPE B.R.I

BRITISH RAILWAYS
LOCOMOTIVE DRAWING OFFICE
DERBY

D.D. 4381

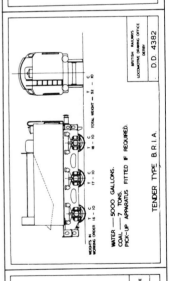

WEIGHTS IN WORKING ORDER 16-10 T C 17-10 T C 18-10 TOTAL WEIGHT 52-80

WATER —— 5000 GALLONS.
COAL —— 7 TONS.
PICK-UP APPARATUS FITTED IF REQUIRED.

TENDER TYPE B.R.I.A.

BRITISH RAILWAYS
LOCOMOTIVE DRAWING OFFICE
D.D. 4382

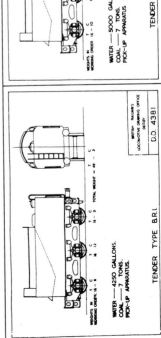

WEIGHTS IN WORKING ORDER 17-5 T C 17-1 T C 17-2 TOTAL WEIGHT 51-5

WATER —— 4725 GALLONS.
COAL —— 7 TONS.
PICK-UP APPARATUS FITTED IF REQUIRED.

TENDER TYPE B.R.I.B

BRITISH RAILWAYS
LOCOMOTIVE DRAWING OFFICE
D.D. 4383

WEIGHTS IN WORKING ORDER 17-18 T C 17-5 T C 17-12 TOTAL WEIGHT 63-5

WATER —— 4725 GALLONS.
COAL —— 9 TONS.
PICK-UP APPARATUS FITTED IF REQUIRED.

TENDER TYPE B.R.I.C.

BRITISH RAILWAYS
LOCOMOTIVE DRAWING OFFICE
D.D. 4384

Plate 171

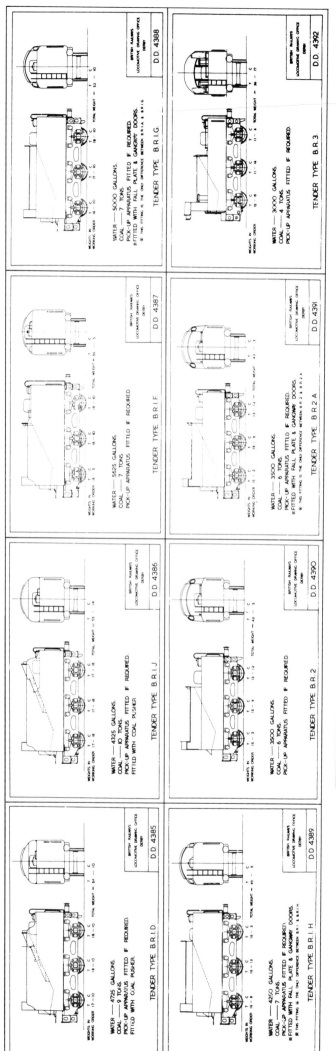

WATER — 5000 GALLONS.
COAL — 7 TONS.
PICK-UP APPARATUS FITTED IF REQUIRED.
※ FITTED WITH FALL PLATE & GANGWAY DOORS.
※ THIS FITTING IS THE ONLY DIFFERENCE BETWEEN B.R.1.A. & B.R.1.G.

TENDER TYPE B.R.1.G.

D.D. 4388

BRITISH RAILWAYS
LOCOMOTIVE DRAWING OFFICE
DERBY

WATER — 3000 GALLONS.
COAL — 4 TONS.
PICK-UP APPARATUS FITTED IF REQUIRED.

TENDER TYPE B.R.3.

D.D. 4392

BRITISH RAILWAYS
LOCOMOTIVE DRAWING OFFICE
DERBY

WATER — 5625 GALLONS.
COAL — 7 TONS.
PICK-UP APPARATUS FITTED IF REQUIRED.

TENDER TYPE B.R.1.F.

D.D. 4387

BRITISH RAILWAYS
LOCOMOTIVE DRAWING OFFICE
DERBY

WATER — 3500 GALLONS.
COAL — 6 TONS.
PICK-UP APPARATUS FITTED IF REQUIRED.
※ FITTED WITH FALL PLATE & GANGWAY DOORS.
※ THIS FITTING IS THE ONLY DIFFERENCE BETWEEN B.R.2 & B.R.2.A.

TENDER TYPE B.R.2.A.

D.D. 4391

BRITISH RAILWAYS
LOCOMOTIVE DRAWING OFFICE
DERBY

WATER — 4325 GALLONS.
COAL — 10 TONS.
PICK-UP APPARATUS FITTED IF REQUIRED.
FITTED WITH COAL PUSHER.

TENDER TYPE B.R.1.J.

D.D. 4386

BRITISH RAILWAYS
LOCOMOTIVE DRAWING OFFICE
DERBY

WATER — 3500 GALLONS.
COAL — 6 TONS.
PICK-UP APPARATUS FITTED IF REQUIRED.

TENDER TYPE B.R.2.

D.D. 4390

BRITISH RAILWAYS
LOCOMOTIVE DRAWING OFFICE
DERBY

WATER — 4725 GALLONS.
COAL — 9 TONS.
PICK-UP APPARATUS FITTED IF REQUIRED.
FITTED WITH COAL PUSHER.

TENDER TYPE B.R.1.D.

D.D. 4385

BRITISH RAILWAYS
LOCOMOTIVE DRAWING OFFICE
DERBY

WATER — 4250 GALLONS.
COAL — 7 TONS.
PICK-UP APPARATUS FITTED IF REQUIRED.
※ FITTED WITH FALL PLATE & GANGWAY DOORS.
※ THIS FITTING IS THE ONLY DIFFERENCE BETWEEN B.R.1 & B.R.1.H.

TENDER TYPE B.R.1.H.

D.D. 4389

BRITISH RAILWAYS
LOCOMOTIVE DRAWING OFFICE
DERBY

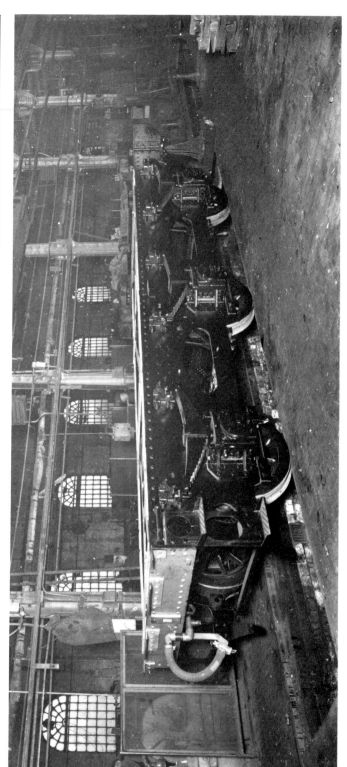

Plate 172 Frame for a 9F tender in
the Tender Shop at Crewe Works.

Plate 173 The last tender built at Crewe, type **BR 1G**, for No. 92250. This view clearly shows the re-designed arrangement of the front of the standard tender, with the short full-width fall-plate to rest on the engine footplate, the shovelling plate above it and the gangway doors (folded back in this picture) with anti-draught flaps fixed to their lower edge.

British Rail

Plate 174 A rear view of the last tender built at Crewe Works. By coincidence, the last engine built at Crewe, No. 92250, had the same type of tender as the first of the class, No. 92000, even down to the Western Region lamp-irons.

British Rail

Appendix Two

Liveries

Soon after British Railways were formed, trials were held with a variety of locomotive and carriage liveries with a view to establishing the future standards. The locomotive liveries consisted of blue, green and black, with different styles of lining. As a result of the trials, it was announced early in 1949 that the most powerful express passenger engines were to be blue, with black and white lining, selected express passenger engines were to be green, officially described as 'Dark Brunswick' green, with black and orange lining, other passenger and mixed-traffic engines were to be black, with red, cream and grey lining, and freight engines were to be plain black. The first three of these liveries recalled those of the Caledonian, Great Western and London & North Western Railways respectively.

A short while later the blue livery was abandoned, too soon, in fact, for it to appear on a **BR** Standard engine. However the other three liveries were used by **BR** until the end of steam and were naturally applied to the Standard engines when they appeared. The three Pacific classes were painted in lined green, as 'selected passenger locomotives', although two of them were officially classified as mixed-traffic engines. All the 4-6-0 and 2-6-0 tender engines and all the tank engines were painted lined black and the 9F 2-10-0s were plain black. These liveries were applied with great consistency and uniformity by the various works throughout the regions and there were very few deviations from standard.

In the late 1950s the feeling arose that the nationalised industries would be more efficient if there was less central control, and there was a move to greater regional autonomy. In consequence, the Western Region applied the lined green livery to many classes which had not had it hitherto. Initially, the Standard engines affected by this were only those allocated to the Western Region itself, the Class 5 and 4 4-6-0s, the Class 2 2-6-0s and the Class 3 2-6-2 tanks. Later, Eastleigh also applied this livery to certain of these classes, partly because green engines were transferred to the Southern Region from the Western by changes in regional boundaries, and in the same way, green engines went from the Western Region to the London Midland. Only one other Standard engine was ever painted in the lined green livery, Class 9F 2-10-0 No. 92220 *Evening Star*, which was the last steam engine built for British Railways and the last steam engine built at Swindon. For a 9F 2-10-0 this was quite exceptional as all others were always in plain black.

In the final years of **BR** steam, some engines which entered works for overhaul in the lined green livery re-emerged in an economy livery of plain green with no lining. This happened with both Pacifics and former Western Region engines, and in some cases a plain green engine was matched with a lined green tender. Quite a number of such things occurred at that time which would never have happened if the abandonment of steam had not been imminent. Name and numberplates, for instance, were removed in many cases and were sometimes replaced by wooden replicas of more or less amateurish appearance. For reasons such as this, photographs taken in 1966-8 should be treated with caution and should not necessarily be assumed to show features typical of the whole **BR** steam era.

Cabside numbers on the Standard engines were generally 8 in. high and the class numbers above them were 2in. high. However, engines built or repainted at Darlington or Cowlairs received 10in. numbers, which sometimes were replaced by 8in. ones on repainting at other works. The colour used for numbers is perhaps best described as pale cream and front numberplates and shed plates were picked out in white.

The following notes detail the livery specification laid down by **BR** in 1949, as it applied to the Standard engines:

The 'British Railways' crest to be placed centrally in the appropriate panels, one left-hand and one right-hand, so that the lion faces forward. Position can be varied slightly to avoid bolt or rivet heads.

All locomotives to carry the crest.

Cab roofs and all hand rails to be black.

Buffer beams and casings to be signal red.

Frame extensions, smokeboxes, saddles, outside steam pipes and cylinder clothing to be black in all cases.

Smoke deflectors to be black and unlined.

All parts below the platform angle, such as wheels and axle ends, to be black and unlined. The motion to remain bright.

The exposed parts on tender tops to be black. No lining on rear of tender. All parts below the tender panel to be black and unlined, including wheels, frame cut-outs, etc.

The position of the lining on tender sides varies slightly according to the type of tender.

Plate 174a This photograph shows a sample of lining and crest on No. 80079.

GENERAL DETAILS

STEAM LOCOMOTIVES.

The "British Railways" crest to be placed centrally in the appropriate panels, one left-hand and one right-hand, so that the lion faces forward. Position can be varied slightly if necessary to avoid bolt or rivet heads.

All locomotives to carry the crest.

Cab roofs and all hand-rails to be black.

Buffer beams and casings to be signal red.

Frame extensions, smoke-boxes, saddles, outside steam pipes and cylinder clothing to be black in all cases.

Smoke deflectors to be black and unlined, except in the "Merchant Navy," and "Battle of Britain" classes.

Ex-G.W.R. locomotives and new locomotives built to G.W.R. designs to keep present size and style of cast number plate on cab or bunker sides.

All locomotives to carry cast number plates on the smoke-box door similar in design to that used on former L.M.S.R. locomotives, and in the same position.

Route availability, where applicable, to follow existing practice.

Cast plates for place and date built, tender number and capacity, etc., to remain as on existing locomotives, except that initial of former company to be omitted.

DIESEL AND ELECTRIC LOCOMOTIVES.

Main-line locomotives with cabs at each end; engine numbers to be on each side as near at each end as convenient, with crest in centre.

Main-line and shunting locomotives with single centre or end cabs; engine number on cab side immediately below windows. Crest in centre of bonnet portion. "Built" plates below engine numbers, but no cast number plate on front or rear.

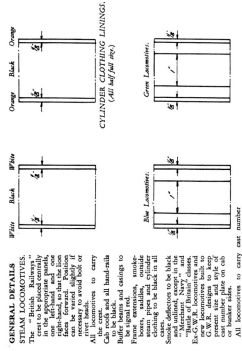

LININGS
FOR
SPLASHERS.
(Half full size.)

Note.—When a splasher has a polished brass beading the top line should be taken from the inside radius of the beading.

Black
Green
Orange

Green Locomotives.

Black
Blue
White

Blue Locomotives.

Note.—When a splasher is extensively screened by external fittings it will probably not be lined.

White   Black   White

Orange   Black   Orange

Red   Black   Red

CYLINDER CLOTHING LININGS.
(All half full size.)

Blue Locomotives.

Green Locomotives.

Black Locomotives.

Red   Black   Red

BOILER CASING BANDS.
(Colours of Blue and Green Locomotives as for linings.)

¼in. Grey
¼in. Cream
¼in. Red
Rest Black

This dimension varies with the size of splasher.

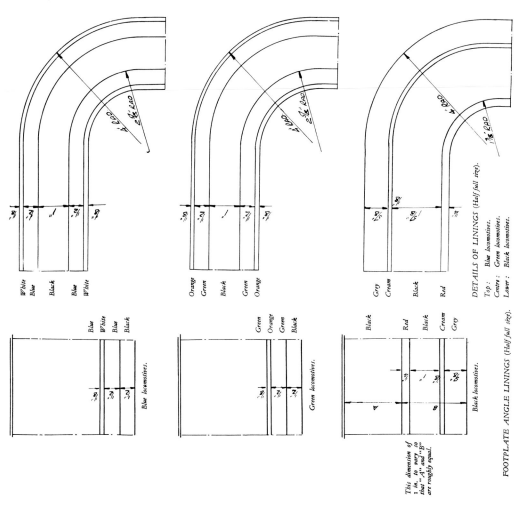

White
Blue
Black
Blue
White

Orange
Green
Black
Green
Orange

Grey
Cream
Black
Red

DETAILS OF LININGS (Half full size).

Top: Blue locomotives.
Centre: Green locomotives.
Lower: Black locomotives.

Blue
White
Blue
Black

Blue locomotives.

Green
Orange
Green
Black

Green locomotives.

Black
Red
Black
Cream
Grey

This dimension of 1 in. to vary, so that "A" and "B" are roughly equal.

Black locomotives.

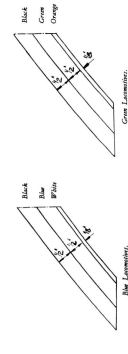

FOOTPLATE ANGLE LININGS (Half full size).

All parts below the platform angle to be black and unlined; this applies particularly to wheels, axle ends, etc., which may have been previously painted otherwise. The motion to remain bright.

The exposed parts on tender tops to be black. No lining on rear of tender. All parts below the tender panel to be black and unlined. This applies particularly to wheels, frame cut-outs, etc., which may have been previously painted otherwise. The position of the lining on tender sides varies slightly according to the type of tender, but is normally as on cab side panels.

Plate 175 Reproduced from official British Rail Drawing.

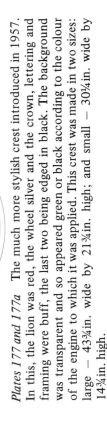

Plates 177 and 177a The much more stylish crest introduced in 1957. In this, the lion was red, the wheel silver and the crown, lettering and framing were buff, the last two being edged in black. The background was transparent and so appeared green or black according to the colour of the engine to which it was applied. This crest was made in two sizes: large — 43¾in. wide by 21¾in. high; and small — 30¾in. wide by 14¾in. high.

Plates 176 and 176a The first British Railways emblem, introduced in mid-1948. Its design was based on the British Transport Commission seal. The lion was chrome yellow lined in red, the wheel was red and white and the title panel was black and white. It was produced in three sizes to suit the area of locomotive side, tender or tank to which it was to be applied: large — 26½in. wide by 28in. high; standard — 15in. wide by 15½in. high; and small — 8½in. wide by 9in. high.

Appendix Three   *Numbers, Numberplates, Nameplates, Tender plates and Shed plates*

Plate 178 (top left) BR standard numerals as used in appropriate sizes not only painted on cab-sides but on all plates, numberplates, shed plates and so forth. There was no '9' as it was the same as the '6' (but upside down, of course!). Most works used 8in. high numerals for cab-side numbers but there were some variations. Swindon used 9in. and Darlington and Cowlairs 10in., while Doncaster appears to have used 8in. for Class 4 2-6-0s and 10in. for Class 5s, 2-6-4 tanks and 9Fs.

Plate 179 (left) A typical standard smokebox numberplate. These plates measured 24in. long by 5.7/8in. wide but as they were fairly rough iron castings, there was no need for critical accuracy and variations of up to 1/8in. were common. The numerals were 4.7/8in. high.

Plate 180 (above) A typical standard shed plate, 7¼in. wide with numerals 2in. high.

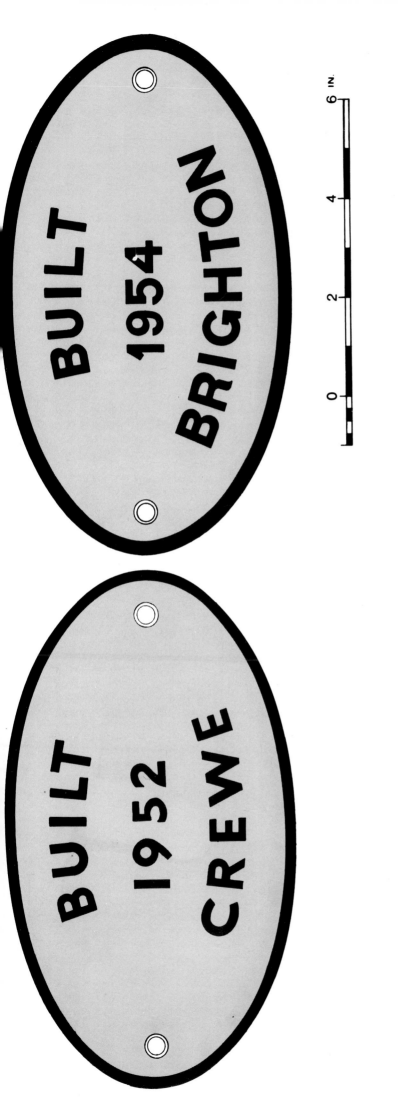

Plates 181 and 182 (above) Works plates were 10½in. long by 6in. wide, and were supposedly standard, with numerals (for the date) 13/16in. high, but there were slight variations of detail, as these two examples show. Preserved engines, incidentally, are not necessarily a good guide, as they often carry inaccurate replica plates. Works plates were made for Crewe, Derby, Horwich, Swindon, Brighton, Doncaster and Darlington.

Plate 183 (left) A standard water capacity plate 10½in. long by 6in. high, with numerals 1½in. high. Plates were made for 5,625, 5,000, 4,725, 4,425, 4,325, 4,250, 3,500, 3,000, 2,000, 1,500 and 1,350 gallons.

CLAN FRASER

CAMELOT

12 IN 6 0

EVENING STAR

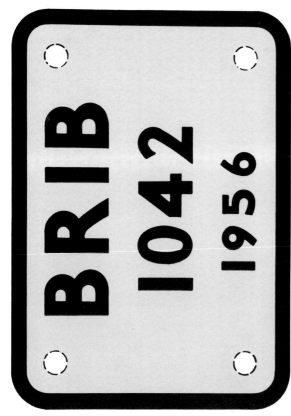

BRIB
1042
1956

Plate 184 (above) A typical tender numberplate, 8in. long by 6in. wide, with numerals 1.1/8in high for the number and ¾in. high for the date.

Plates 185 and 186 (above) Typical nameplates, of varying length according to the name. The Standard type originally was that used on all the Pacifics and was fastened to the smoke deflectors. When some of the Southern's Standard Class 5s were named, their nameplates followed the design of those on the Southern Railway's 'King Arthurs'. Finally, the nameplates of *Evening Star* were different again, being cast in brass in a style similar to those of the Pacifics but with GWR style letters.   *All drawings: Alan Gettings*

Plate 187 This shows the nameplate and building plate of *Evening Star*.

British Rail

EVENING STAR

N° 92220 BUILT AT SWINDON
MARCH 1960

THE LAST STEAM LOCOMOTIVE FOR BRITISH RAILWAYS
NAMED AT SWINDON ON MARCH 18TH 1960 BY
K.W.C. GRAND ESQ
MEMBER OF THE BRITISH TRANSPORT COMMISSION

Appendix Four

List of BR Standard Steam Engines

'Britannia' Class 7 4-6-2

Nos.	Annual programme	Built at	Building dates	Tender type	Tender Nos.	Region allocated
70000-70014	1951	Crewe	1/51-6/51	1	759-773	E
70015-70024	"	"	6/51-10/51	1	774-783	W
70025-70029	1952	"	9/52-11/52	1A	844-848	W
70030-70034	"	"	11/52-12/52	1	849-853	LM
70035-70044	"	"	12/52-6/53	1	854-863	E
70045-70049	1953	"	6/54-7/54	1D	979-983	LM
70050-70054	"	"	7/54-9/54	1D	984-988	Sc
73080-73089	"	"	6/55-9/55	1B	1206-1215	S
73090-73099	1955	"	10/55-12/55	1C	1272-1281	LM
73100-73109	"	Doncaster	8/55-1/56	1B	1282-1291	Sc
73110-73119	"	"	10/55-12/55	1F	1292-1301	S
73120-73124	"	"	1/56-2/56	1B	1302-1306	Sc
73125-73134*	1956	Derby	7/56-10/56	1B	1413-1422	W
73135-73144*	"	"	10/56-12/56	1C	1423-1432	LM
73145-73154*	"	"	1/57-6/57	1B	1433-1442	Sc
73155-73159	"	Doncaster	12/56-1/57	1B	1443-1447	E
73160-73171	"	"	1/57-5/57	1B	1448-1459	NE

Total: 55

* Fitted with British-Caprotti valve gear.

Total: 172

Class 8 4-6-2

No.	Annual programme	Built at	Building date	Tender type	Tender Nos.	Region allocated
71000	*	Crewe	5/54	1E/1J	1271/1528	LM

Total: 1

* Authorised as replacement for No. 46202 *Princess Anne*; not part of any annual programme.

'Clan' Class 6 4-6-2

Nos.	Annual programme	Built at	Building date	Tender type	Tender Nos.	Region allocated
72000-72009	1951	Crewe	12/51-3/52	1	784-793	Sc
72010-72014	1952	"	Cancelled			S
72015-72024	"	"	"			Sc

Total: 10

Class 5 4-6-0

Nos.	Annual programme	Built at	Building dates	Tender type	Tender Nos.	Region allocated
73000-73004	1951	Derby	4/51-6/51	1	794-798	LM
73005-73009	"	"	6/51-7/51	1	799-803	Sc
73010-73029	"	"	9/51-1/52	1	804-823	LM
73030-73039	1952	"	6/53-9/53	1	864-873	Sc
73040-73049	"	"	10/53-12/53	1	874-883	LM
73050-73052	1953	"	4/54-5/54	1G	989-991	S
73053-73054	"	"	6/54	1H	992-993	LM
73055-73064	"	"	6/54-10/54	1H	994-1003	Sc
73065-73074	"	"	10/54-12/54	1C	1004-1013	LM
73075-73079	1954	"	4/55-5/55	1C	1014-1018	Sc

Class 4 4-6-0

Nos.	Annual programme	Built at	Building dates	Tender type	Tender Nos.	Region allocated
75000-75009	1951	Swindon	5/51-10/51	2	824-833	W
75010-75019	"	"	11/51-3/52	"	834-843	LM
75020-75029	1952	"	11/53-5/54	"	884-893	W
75030-75049	"	"	7/53-10/53	"	894-913	LM
75050-75064	1953	"	11/56-7/57	2A	1014-1028	LM
75065-75079	"	"	8/55-1/56	1B	1029-1043	S
75080-75089	1954	"	Cancelled			E

Total: 80

Class 4 2-6-0

Nos.	Annual programme	Built at	Building dates	Tender type	Tender Nos.	Region allocated
76000-76004	1952	Horwich	12/52	2	914-918	Sc
76005-76019	"	"	12/52-7/53	"	919-933	S
76020-76024	"	Doncaster	12/52-1/53	"	934-938	NE
76025-76029	1953	"	10/53-11/53	"	1044-1048	S
76030-76044	"	"	11/53-8/54	"	1049-1063	E
76045-76052	1954	"	3/55-9/56	2A	1226-1233	NE
76053-76069	"	"	4/55-8/56	1B	1234-1250	S
76070-76074	"	"	9/56-11/56	2A	1251-1255	Sc
76075-76089	1956	Horwich	12/56-6/57	"	1460-1474	LM
76090-76099	"	"	6/57-11/57	"	1475-1484	Sc
76100-76114	"	Doncaster	5/57-10/57	"	1485-1499	Sc

Total: 115

Class 3 2-6-0

Nos.	Annual programme	Built at	Building dates	Tender type	Tender Nos.	Region allocated
77000-77004	1953	Swindon	2/54-3/54	2A	1064-1068	NE
77005-77009	"	"	3/54-6/54	"	1069-1073	Sc
77010-77014	"	"	6/54-7/54	"	1074-1078	NE
77015-77019	"	"	7/54-9/54	"	1079-1083	Sc

Total: 20

Class 2 2-6-0

Nos.	Annual programme	Built at	Building dates	Tender type	Tender Nos.	Region allocated
78000-78009	1952	Darlington	12/52-4/53	3	939-948*	W
78010-78019	1953	"	12/53-3/54	"	1084-1093	NE
78020-78044	"	"	4/54-12/54	"	1094-1118	LM
78045-78054	1954	"	10/55-12/55	"	1261-1270	Sc
78055-78064	1956	"	8/56-11/56	"	1500-1509	LM

Total: 65

Class 4 2-6-4T

Nos.	Annual programme	Built at	Building dates	Region allocated
80000-80009	1951	Derby	9/52-12/52	Sc
80010-80019	"	Brighton	7/51-10/51	S
80020-80030	"	"	10/51 2/52	Sc
80031-80033	"	"	2/52-3/52	NE
80034-80053	"	"	4/52-12/52	LM
80054-80058	1952	Derby	11/54-1/55	Sc
80059-80068	"	Brighton	3/53-8/53	LM
80069-80080	1953	"	9/53-3/54	E
80081-80095	"	"	4/54-11/54	LM
80096-80105	"	"	11/54-4/55	E
80106-80115	"	Doncaster	10/54 12/54	Sc
80116-80120	1954	Brighton	5/55-7/55	NE
80121-80130	"	"	8/55-12/55	Sc
80131-80144	1956	"	3/56-9/56	E
80145-80154	"	"	10/56-3/57	S

Total: 155

Class 3 2-6-2T

Nos.	Annual programme	Built at	Building dates	Region allocated
82000-82009	1951	Swindon	4/52-6/52	W
82010-82019	"	"	6/52-9/52	S
82020-82029	1952	"	9/54-12/54	S
82030-82034	"	"	12/54-1/55	W
82035-82044	1953	"	3/55-8/55	W
82045-82054	1954	"	Cancelled	W
82055-82062	"	"	"	NE

Total: 45

Class 2 2-6-2T

Nos.	Annual programme	Built at	Building dates	Region allocated
84000-84019	1952	Crewe	7/53-10/53	LM
84020-84029	1953	Darlington	3/57-6/57	S

Total: 30

Class 9F 2-10-0

Nos.	Annual programme	Built at	Building dates	Tender type	Tender Nos.	Region allocated
92000-92007	1953	Crewe	1/54-2/54	1G	949-956	W
92008-92009	"	"	3/54	"	957-958	LM
92010-92014	"	"	4/54-5/54	1F	959-963	E
92015-92019	"	"	9/54-10/54	1C	964-968	LM
92020-92029	"	"	5/55-7/55	1B	969-978	LM
92030-92044	1954	"	11/54-1/55	1F	1119-1133	E
92045-92059	"	"	2/55-10/55	1C	1134-1148	LM
92060-92066	"	"	11/55-12/55	1B	1149-1155	NE
92067-92076	"	"	12/55-3/56	1F	1156-1165	E
92077-92086	"	"	3/56-6/56	1C	1166-1175	LM
92087-92096	"	"	8/56-4/57	1F	1176-1185	E
92097-92099	1956	"	6/56-7/56	1B	1307-1309	NE
92100-92139	"	"	8/56-7/57	1C	1310-1349	LM
92140-92149	"	"	7/57-10/57	1F	1350-1359	E
92150-92164	"	"	10/57-4/58	1C	1271, 1361-1373	LM
92165-92167	"	"	4/58-6/58	1C	1529-1531	LM
92168-92177	"	"	12/57-3/58	1K	1378-1387	E
92178-92202	"	Swindon	9/57-12/58	1F	1388-1412	E
92203-92220	1957	"	4/59-3/60	1F	1510-1527	W
92221-92250	"	Crewe	5/58-12/58	1G	1532-1561	W

Total: 251

Total tender engines: 769
Total tank engines: 230

* Engine record cards show that in fact these tenders were fitted out of order. For example, 78000 had 944, 78002 had 941, 78003 had 942 and 78008 had 947.

70000 Britannia
70001 Lord Hurcomb
70002 Geoffrey Chaucer
70003 John Bunyan
70004 William Shakespeare
70005 John Milton
70006 Robert Burns
70007 Coeur-de-Lion
70008 Black Prince
70009 Alfred the Great
70010 Owen Glendower
70011 Hotspur
70012 John of Gaunt
70013 Oliver Cromwell

70014 Iron Duke
70015 Apollo
70016 Ariel
70017 Arrow
70018 Flying Dutchman
70019 Lightning
70020 Mercury
70021 Morning Star
70022 Tornado
70023 Venus
70024 Vulcan
70025 Western Star
70026 Polar Star
70027 Rising Star

70028 Royal Star
70029 Shooting Star
70030 William Wordsworth
70031 Byron
70032 Tennyson
70033 Charles Dickens
70034 Thomas Hardy
70035 Rudyard Kipling
70036 Boadicea
70037 Hereward the Wake
70038 Robin Hood
70039 Sir Christopher Wren
70040 Clive of India
70041 Sir John Moore

70042 Lord Roberts
70043 Lord Kitchener
70044 Earl Haig
70045 Lord Rowallan
70046 Anzac
70047 —
70048 The Territorial Army
       1908-1958
70049 Solway Firth
70050 Firth of Clyde
70051 Firth of Forth
70052 Firth of Tay
70053 Mornay Firth
70054 Dornoch Firth

71000 Duke of Gloucester

The names for the 'Clan' Class which were not built were:-

72010 Hengist
72011 Horsa
72012 Canute
72013 Wildfire
72014 Firebrand
72015 Clan Colquhoun
72016 Clan Graham
72017 Clan MacDougall

72018 Clan Maclean
72019 Clan Douglas
72020 Clan Gordon
72021 Clan Hamilton
72022 Clan Kennedy
72023 Clan Lindsay
72024 Clan Scott

72000 Clan Buchanan
72001 Clan Cameron
72003 Clan Campbell
72004 Clan Fraser
72005 Clan Macdonald

72005 Clan Macgregor
72006 Clan Mackenzie
72007 Clan Mackintosh
72008 Clan Macleod
72009 Clan Stewart

92220 Evening Star

73080 Merlin
73081 Excalibur
73082 Camelot
73083 Pendragon
73084 Tintagel
73085 Melisande
73086 The Green Knight
73087 Linette
73088 Joyous Gard
73089 Maid of Astolat

73110 The Red Knight
73111 King Uther
73112 Morgan le Fay
73113 Lyonesse
73114 Etarre
73115 King Pellinore
73116 Iseult
73117 Vivien
73118 King Leodegrance
73119 Elaine

Appendix Six

Proposed Designs

Plate 188 The original proposal for a Class 9 heavy freight engine envisaged a 2-8-2, using the 'Britannia' boiler and 5 ft. driving wheels to give an increase in speed over existing Class 8 2-8-0s. R. A. Riddles, however, favoured the superior adhesion of the 2-10-0 wheel arrangement, particularly for a freight engine, and eventually a wide firebox 2-10-0 with 5 ft. driving wheels was designed within the L2 loading gauge. The Class 9F 2-10-0 was the result and although the boiler was not standard with any other class, the performance of the engine in service amply justified Riddles' decision.

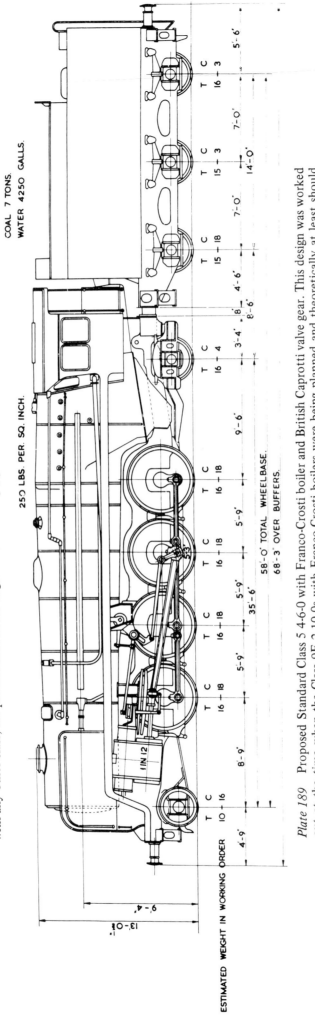

Plate 189 Proposed Standard Class 5 4-6-0 with Franco-Crosti boiler and British Caprotti valve gear. This design was worked out at the time when the Class 9F 2-10-0s with Franco-Crosti boilers were being planned and theoretically at least should have proved extremely efficient. However, the difficulties with the boilers on the 9Fs ensured that no such engines were ever built.

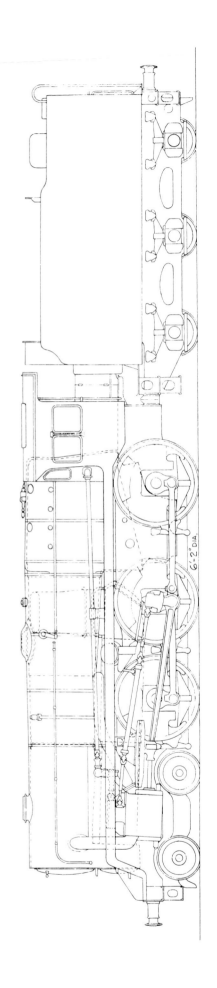

Appendix Seven

Engines Preserved and Bibliography

Class		No.	Name	Location
7	4-6-2	70000	*Britannia*	Nene Valley Railway, Peterborough
7	4-6-2	70013	*Oliver Cromwell*	Bressingham Hall, Diss
8	4-6-2	71000	*Duke of Gloucester*	Main Line Steam Trust, Loughborough
5	4-6-0	73050	*City of Peterborough**	Nene Valley Railway, Peterborough
5	4-6-0	73082	*Camelot*	Bluebell Railway
5	4-6-0	73129		Midland Railway Co., Butterley
4	4-6-0	75014		North Yorkshire Moors Railway
4	4-6-0	75027		Bluebell Railway
4	4-6-0	75029	*The Green Knight**	East Somerset Railway
4	4-6-0	75069		Severn Valley Railway
4	4-6-0	75078		Keighley & Worth Valley Railway
4	2-6-0	76017		Mid Hants Railway, Alresford
4	2-6-0	76079		Steamport, Southport
2	2-6-0	78018		Market Bosworth Light Railway
2	2-6-0	78019		Severn Valley Railway
2	2-6-0	78022		Keighley & Worth Valley Railway
4	2-6-4T	80002		Keighley & Worth Valley Railway
4	2-6-4T	80064		Swanage Railway Society
4	2-6-4T	80078		Southern Steam Trust, Swanage
4	2-6-4T	80079		Severn Valley Railway
4	2-6-4T	80100		Bluebell Railway
4	2-6-4T	80104		Southern Steam Trust, Swanage
4	2-6-4T	80105		Scottish RPS, Falkirk
4	2-6-4T	80135		North Yorkshire Moors Railway
4	2-6-4T	80136		North Staffordshire Railway, Cheddleton
4	2-6-4T	80151		Stour Valley Railway
9F	2-10-0	92134		North Yorkshire Moors Railway
9F	2-10-0	92203	*Black Prince**	East Somerset Railway
9F	2-10-0	92212		Great Central Railway, Loughborough
9F	2-10-0	92214		Peak Railway Society, Buxton
9F	2-10-0	92220	*Evening Star*	National Railway Museum, York
9F	2-10-0	92240		Bluebell Railway

* So named only since preservation, not by BR.

Bibliography

The following books are recommended as further sources of information on BR Standard steam engines:

Bond, Roland C. *A Lifetime with Locomotives* Goose & Son

Cox, E. S. *British Railways Standard Steam Locomotives* Ian Allan

Cox, E. S. *Chronicles of Steam* Ian Allan

Cox, E. S. *Locomotive Panorama (Vol. 2)* Ian Allan

Haresnape, B. *Ivatt and Riddles Locomotives* Ian Allan

Reed, B. *Loco Profile 12, BR Britannias* Profile Publications

Reed, B. *Loco Profile 33, Class 9 2-10-0s* Profile Publications

Rogers, Colonel H. C. B. *The Last Steam Locomotive Engineer: R. A. Riddles CBE* George Allen & Unwin

Weekes, G. *BR Standard Britannia Pacifics* Bradford Barton

Weekes, G. *BR Standard 2-10-0s Class 9F* Bradford Barton

Whiteley, J. S. and Morrison, G. W. *Power of the BR Standard Pacifics* Oxford Publishing Co.

Part Two

BRITISH RAILWAYS STANDARDS IN SERVICE

THE EARLY YEARS

Plate 190 As the latest express engines, certain 'Britannias' were put to work on trains which were particularly in the public eye. Three went to the Southern Region, Nos. 70004 and 70014 for the 'Golden Arrow', and No. 70009 for the 'Royal Wessex'. Here, No. 70004 *William Shakespeare* is seen suitably decorated with the 'Arrow' near Folkestone in March 1952.   *A. G. Ellis Collection*

Plate 191 The majority of the first batch of 'Britannias' went to East Anglia where they revolutionised express services to Liverpool Street. Here, No. 70007 *Coeur de Lion* leaves Ipswich with 'The East Anglian' on 8th October, 1952.

A. G. Ellis Collection

Plate 192 No. 80009 at Corkerhill on 5th June, 1954. It is well cared for, in a manner typical of certain ex-LMS sheds in Scotland, with various parts of the front end of the engine in a light colour, probably pale (Caledonian) blue.

A. G. Ellis Collection

Plate 194 No. 73006, still quite new, climbing past St. Rollox shed with the 12.20pm from Glasgow Buchanan Street on 3rd November, 1951.

A. G. Ellis Collection

Plate 193 No. 70022 *Tornado* at Teignmouth on the up 'Devonian', 2nd August, 1955.

A. G. Ellis Collection

Plate 195 No. 80115 on a Glasgow suburban passenger train at Paisley on 21st March, 1955. Being a Doncaster-built engine, it has larger numerals and an 'R.A.' number on the cab-side, and its class on the bufferbeam. Above the latter is a Caledonian route indicator, and the smokebox has typical Scottish decorations.
A. G. Ellis Collection

Plate 196 A summer scene on the Southern, with No. 80015 on an Oxted line passenger train in the mid-1950s.
A. G. Ellis Collection

Plate 197 The Standard Class 5s also worked regularly on the Southern's main lines to Dover and Ramsgate via both Chatham and Ashford before those lines were electrified. Here, No. 73085 is seen with a Pullman train, presumably 'The Kentish Belle', near Birchington-on-Sea, west of Margate in September 1959.

Dawlish Warren Railway Museum

Plate 198 No. 73085 at Surbiton with an up semi-fast to Waterloo in May 1962. This was a typical working for a Standard Class 5 on the South Western section.

Author

Plate 199 'Clan' No. 72004 *Clan MacDonald* on a down summer Saturday relief near Crawford on the Caledonian main line on 14th July, 1962.

G. W. Morrison

Plate 200 No. 73055 climbing Shap on a Manchester-Glasgow express on 7th July, 1956.

A. G. Ellis Collection

Plate 201 A fine sight at Colwyn Bay in 1956, as No. 70048, still un-named, sweeps through on the up 'Irish Mail' loaded to 15 bogies. Such loads were commonplace, up to the early 1960s, on expresses using the West Coast route.

Author's Collection

Plate 202 The up 'Cambrian Coast Express' climbing Talerddig bank behind two Class 4 4-6-0s on 26th September, 1959.

Author

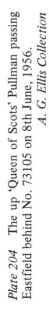

Plate 203 The Standard Class 2 2-6-0s took over many of the duties which at one time had been handled by the redundant main-line engines such as 2-4-0s and 4-4-0s. A typical example is inspection saloon duty on which No. 78049 is here seen employed at Innerwick in March 1956.

A. G. Ellis Collection

Plate 204 The up 'Queen of Scots' Pullman passing Eastfield behind No. 73105 on 8th June, 1956.

A. G. Ellis Collection

Plate 205 No. 82004 at Staple Hill on a Bristol-Bath local in the late 1950s.

Dawlish Warren Railway Museum

Plate 206 No. 84022 in wintry conditions near Sturry, Kent, in January 1959.
Dawlish Warren Railway Museum

9Fs NATIONWIDE

Plate 207 No. 92130 on the up slow line at Bushey in June 1962. Except for the first four wagons, the load consists entirely of coal from East Midland pits to London. Through workings from the Midland to the LNWR main line date back well before the Grouping to the turn of the century, if not beyond.
Author

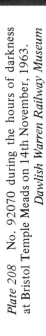

Plate 208 No. 92070 during the hours of darkness at Bristol Temple Meads on 14th November, 1963.
Dawlish Warren Railway Museum

Plate 209 No. 92079 replaced 'Big Bertha', the Midland 0-10-0 numbered 58100 by **BR**, as the Lickey banker, and is seen here about to drop away from an express as it tops the summit at Blackwell. The cover of the water-filler on the tender has been left open – a frequent occurrence.
G. W. Morrison

Plate 210 It was on the Great Northern main line that the 9Fs astounded officials and enthusiasts alike by their speedy running on expresses. Here, more typically on an up fast freight, No. 92141 passes High Dyke on the long climb to Stoke Summit.

G. W. Morrison

Plate 211 No. 92068 on the Great Central main line with an up freight. The 9Fs were used in some numbers to accelerate freight working between Annesley and Woodford Halse.

OPC Collection

Plate 212 No. 92048 leaves Neville Hill yard on an oil train on 29th April, 1967. *G. W. Morrison*

Plate 213 A 9F at Tyne Dock on 18th March, 1964. Once all its bogie hopper wagons are loaded with iron ore, it will start the heavy slog up to Consett.

G. W. Morrison

Plate 214 No. 92184 passes Newcastle Central on an up fast freight which it has collected at Heaton, and sets off for London in June 1963. Despite its unofficial name, it will doubtless handle the train very competently. *Author*

Plate 215 An all-Standard line-up at Bournemouth Central shed on Sunday, 31st July, 1966. From right to left are seen Nos. 80146, 73117, 76057, 76033, 76006 and 73002. Such crowded scenes were typical of steam sheds on Sundays. *G. W. Morrison*

Plate 216 The shed at Ayr on Sunday, 18th May, 1958, with from left to right, Nos. 13006, 45121 (from Motherwell), 80030 and 80009 (both from Corkerhill), and 13005.
G. W. Morrison

THE SOMERSET AND DORSET

Plate 217 The 9Fs were eventually banned from express passenger work on the main lines by the imposition of a 60mph limit but they continued to be so used on the Somerset & Dorset where they proved themselves the best engines ever to have worked over that notoriously difficult line. Even there, however, they were only allowed to haul passenger trains in summer as none of the class were ever fitted with steam carriage-heating apparatus. Here, No. 92001 passes Bath Junction with the 7.45am from Bradford to Bournemouth on 14th July, 1962. The catcher is extended to collect the tablet for the single-line section.
Hugh Ballantyne

Plate 218 A Bournemouth-Leeds express enters Wellow station, on 28th July, 1962, double-headed by Nos. 75072 and 73047. A typical summer Saturday combination.

G. W. Morrison

Plate 219 No. 80041 leaves Sturminster Newton on 30th December, 1965 with a Templecombe to Bournemouth West local passenger service.

G. W. Morrison

Plate 220 No. 76068 approaching Branksome with a down local freight on 31st August, 1965.

G. W. Morrison

Plate 221 A freight sets off from Stainmore Summit for West Auckland behind two Class 2 2-6-0s on 16th August, 1958. The leading engine, No. 78017, had banked the train up from Kirkby Stephen and ran round to the front of the train at Stainmore to double-head No. 78013 for the long descent to Bowes and Barnard Castle.   *G. W. Morrison*

THE STAINMORE LINE

Plate 222 At the opposite end of the country from the Somerset & Dorset was the equally spectacular, though now comparatively forgotten, line between Kirkby Stephen and Barnard Castle over Stainmore Summit, 1,370 ft. above sea level and the highest point on any railway in England. The largest engines allowed over it were the Class 4 2-6-0s and all three Standard 2-6-0 classes became regular power for the line, often double-headed. Here the last train over the line, an RCTS special, leaves Kirkby Stephen on 20th January, 1962 behind Standard 2-6-0s, Class 3 No. 77003, Class 3 No. 77003, Class 4 No. 76049.   *G. W. Morrison*

Plate 223 The 3.45pm from Glasgow Queen Street to Fort William takes the West Highland line at Craigendoran behind Standard and ex-LMS Class 5s, Nos. 73078 and 44956 on 11th August, 1960.

G. W. Morrison

Plate 224 No. 72001 at Ardlui on 16th June, 1956 with the special train for the 'Clan Cameron Gathering'.
A. G. Ellis Collection

Plate 225 No. 76001 of Motherwell was loaned to Fort William for a time and tried on the Mallaig extension. It is seen here at Lochailort on the 3.15 pm from Fort William to Mallaig on 13th August, 1960.
G. W. Morrison

Plate 226 (left)   No. 80126 takes water at Loch Tay shed on 5th June, 1963.
Author

Plate 227 (above) No. 76104 with a ballast train between Gartly and Huntly on the Great North of Scotland section on 11th June, 1959.
G. W. Morrison

Plate 228 (below) No. 80092 at Stanley Junction with a stopping train on 15th June, 1960.
A. G. Ellis Collection

Plate 229 No. 80121 at Tillynaught Junction with the 3.45 pm from Aberdeen to Elgin.

G. W. Morrison

Plate 230 No. 72007 *Clan Mackintosh* approaching Clifton and Lowther signal box in May 1964 with empty hopper wagons for Shap Quarry. At the quarry they will be loaded with limestone and dispatched to Ravenscraig steelworks, Glasgow.

Author

LIMESTONE TRAFFIC FROM SHAP TO GLASGOW

Plate 231 Clifton and Lowther looking south, as No. 75032 and 92109 double-head a northbound loaded train on 8th September, 1967. The leading engine has a home-made front numberplate and both are in the dirty condition which was sadly typical of the last days of **BR** steam.

L. A. Nixon

Plate 232 Converted Crosti No. 92023 battles up Beattock near Greskine box with a limestone train for Glasgow in May 1964. A 2-6-4 tank helps at the rear.

Author

Plate 233 Towards the end of steam, name and numberplates were generally removed and engines allowed to get into a disreputable state, which would have been rare in the 1950s. Here, No. 70015, formerly *Apollo*, stands on shed at Stockport Edgeley on 15th February, 1966.

L. A. Nixon

Plate 234 No. 70012, once named *John of Gaunt*, in the Lune Gorge with a down goods in the summer of 1967. Today the photographer would have to stand in the middle of the M6 motorway to get a view of the same location.   *L. A. Nixon*

Plate 235 No. 75015 approaching Scale Halt, between Lancaster and Morecambe, on 9th October, 1965, beneath the wires of the 25 kV scheme.
G. W. Morrison

Plate 236 No. 84028 entering Skipton Yard with a freight from Barnoldswick on 3rd March, 1965.
G. W. Morrison

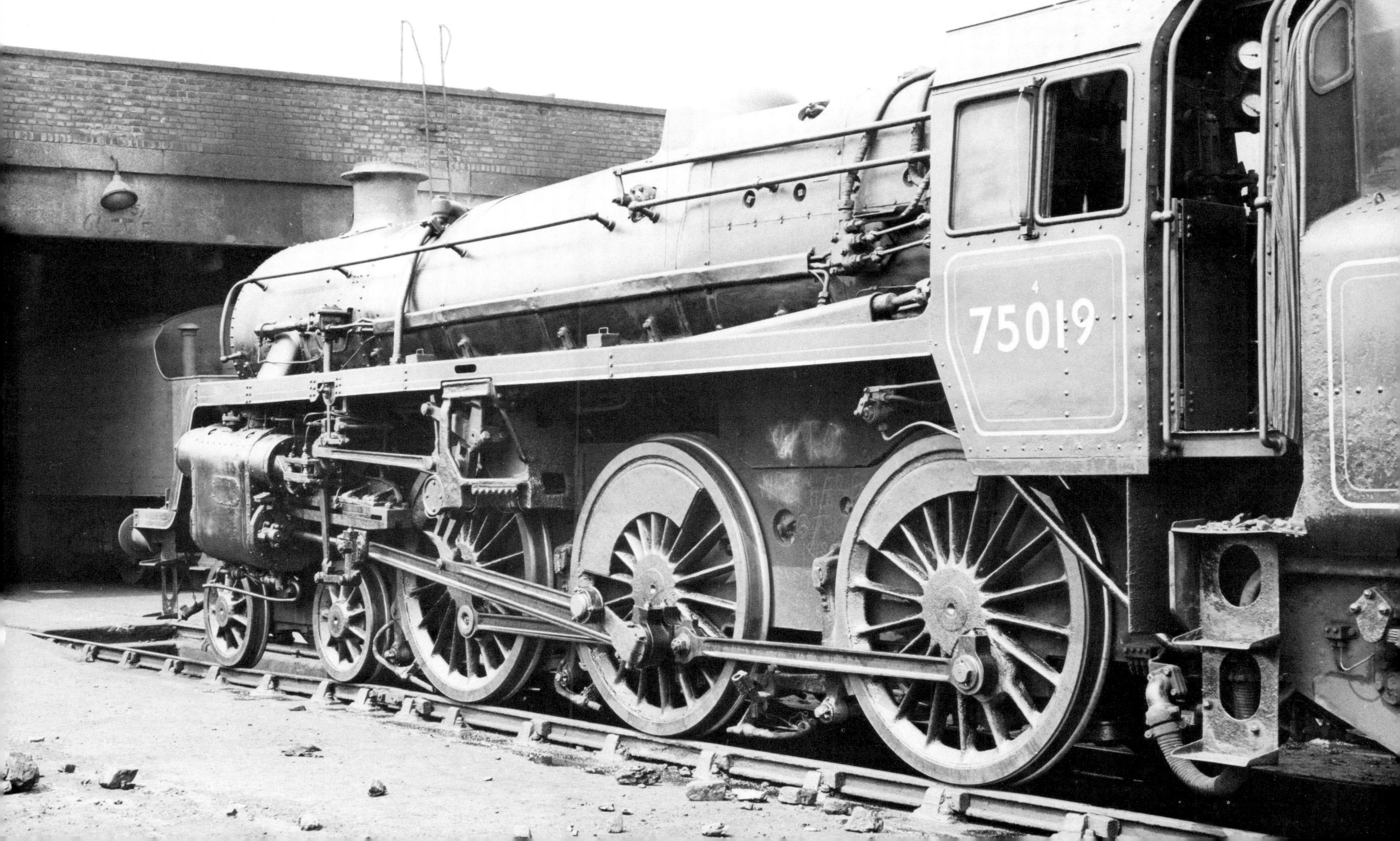

SHED SCENES

Plate 237 No. 75019 at Rose Grove on 15th June, 1968 is surprisingly clean, perhaps having received special treatment for working 'end of steam' specials.

L. A. Nixon

Plate 238 No. 75061 at Chester shed on 4th August, 1966 in the condition typical of the end of steam on **BR** – very dirty, without front numberplate or shedplate, and with the shed code painted on.

L. A. Nixon

Plate 239 Caprotti Class 5 No. 73125 at Patricroft in May 1966. It has a home-made front numberplate, probably of wood, and the shed code is painted on.

L. A. Nixon

Plate 240 A number of enthusiasts' specials ran in the north-west of England at the very end of steam on **BR**. Here, No. 73069 works the LCGB 'Two Cities Limited' over the third rail electrified line at Bootle on 23rd June, 1968.

L. A. Nixon

FINALE

Plate 241 A 9F 2-10-0 restarts a freight train at Hathersage on a cold February morning in 1966.
L. A. Nixon